YOUR GUIDE TO REAL ESTATE INVESTING

By Shelly Roberson and David S. Roberson, Esq.

INTRODUCTION

The real estate investment world can be an overwhelming experience for those who are just getting started. We understand how intimidating it can be to enter this arena. Many of our clients have asked us for a simple book or guide that we could provide them such that they could have a better understanding of real estate investments. We have put together this guide to walk them and you through the basics of investing in real estate and help you make the right choices so you may capitalize on real estate investments for a financially sound future. While this guide is not all-inclusive, it will provide a basic understanding to help you get started from a personal and professional perspective.

What You Will Hopefully Learn

As you read through this guide, you will encounter chapters covering different aspects of real estate investing. With this guidance, you can work toward building financial independence and wealth for your retirement years, and minimizing your risks and failures. In this book, you will learn:

1. How to educate yourself in real estate investing so you have a firm understanding of what is required and what you can expect;

2. Strategies for choosing a niche market so you can focus on one specific area of real estate, rather than diving into all of them in the beginning;

3. How to create an effective real estate business plan to help create a sustainable business that will get through even economic downturns;

4. The best methods for finding ideal investment properties, including the various types of properties you may want to consider;

5. How to get the financing you need to fund your real estate ventures;

6. Strategies for marketing your real estate investment company so you can attract the right people to your business model; and

7. Some varieties of exit and tax strategies and how to execute them so you can minimize your risk, your tax expense, and sell your investments at the appropriate time

Getting Started

While this guide isn't all-encompassing, you will gain a firm understanding of what it means to enter this lucrative industry and generate a passive flow of income you can count on for your future. As you go through this book, we encourage you to keep a list of questions you would like to ask and turn to us for help answering all of these questions. We also encourage you to browse through our websites and read the articles found there to help you make the right decision for your financial future. It's common to feel overwhelmed when you are first exposed to real estate investing, but with the help of this book and access to us you will be ready to invest in properties for long-term gain.

1

THE WORLD OF REAL ESTATE INVESTING

Are you thinking about investing in real estate? For most people, the idea of spending your money on property you won't live in can be overwhelming and may seem expensive or even impossible. This chapter is designed to answer many of the questions most first-time investors have so you can move forward in the decision-making process.

There are Hundreds of Reasons to Invest in Real Estate

One of the first questions potential investors ask is whether it is worth it to invest in real estate. While this answer varies widely depending on your reasons and the work you put in, there are specific reasons individuals choose this path. There are plenty of other options, such as stocks, bonds, currencies, precious metals, commodities and more. So why real estate? Just like any other

investment opportunity, there are pros and cons. We will explore them here.

If you ask anyone why they have decided to invest in real estate, you will get a wide variety of answers. Some of the most common responses to this question include:

1. Generating a steady flow of cash;

2. Creating financial freedom;

3. Receiving tax benefits; and

4. Taking advantage of the increasing value of property.

Choosing to invest in real estate is a highly personal decision. Before making a final choice, it's important to discuss your reasons and the various options available with the entire family, as well as anyone else who will be involved, to ensure everyone is on the same page.

Investing in Real Estate with a Full-Time Job

It can be intimidating to think about quitting your full-time job to give real estate investing your full attention. This leads many potential investors to ask the question whether they can get started, while still working their current job. The answer is yes. You don't have to spend all of your waking hours searching for homes to buy and overseeing maintenance and renovation projects like you see on television programs.

There are hundreds of ways you can make money in the real estate game. While some of these methods may require your full attention, there are other investment opportunities that require little time commitment so you can continue to work until you are on solid footing in the world of real estate. The amount of time you need to dedicate depends greatly on what you want to accomplish, as well as your own knowledge, skills, and personality.

Have you ever wondered what you would do if you won the lottery and didn't have to work any longer? Most people would get bored sitting around home watching television all day. When you answer this question, you will have your answer to what you should do with your life. If real estate isn't your passion, you can still invest, but it isn't going to be something you want to spend all your time doing. The good news is you can still bring in a steady flow of reliable income without quitting your full-time job to do it.

The Advantages of This Strategy

There are distinct advantages to investing in real estate on a part-time basis while maintaining full-time employment. First and foremost, you don't have to be concerned about making enough money to maintain your household. This allows you to reinvest some or all of the funds you make into new ventures so you can continue to grow a sustainable business. You will also be able to obtain funding more easily because you have a steady income to provide the collateral lending institutions are looking for.

If you want to attempt working full time and investing in real estate part time, there are several ways to do it. You can:

1. Buy property and allow a property management firm to handle it;

2. Partner into a larger property holding firm;

3. Buy Portions of Real Estate Investment Trusts (REIT)

4. Invest in mortgages; or

5. Serve as a private lender, if you have the funds.

While real estate can be a lucrative career on its own, it also makes a great supplemental source of income. It all depends on the work you are willing to put in and what you want to achieve from your investments. It's rarely a good idea to quit your "day" job and dive into the world of real estate investing without first testing the water and building a solid foundation. What you choose to do after that is up to you.

Everyone wants a career they are excited to work in every day. Whether real estate is that passion or you just need something on the side to help bolster your finances, real estate investments can be beneficial because you aren't just building a career, you're building a future.

'Rich Dad Poor Dad' Is a Must-Read

Robert Kiyosaki authored "Rich Dad, Poor Dad" which is a very good book to begin thinking about investment properties – as it allows basic information to resonate and create a mindset capable of understanding the power of leverage and owning rental property. Kiyosaki has written a series of "Rich Dad…" books – do yourself a favor and order this book and read it. You will instantly see the value in this small investment.

Getting Professional Help is a Good Practice

Real estate investment professionals want people to think they can't make money in this business without having someone with extensive knowledge to help. Unfortunately, these individuals are more concerned with building their own wealth than in helping people truly get started investing in real estate. They prey on people who are eager to make money by offering boot camps, training courses and more, all with a hefty price tag. If it sounds too good to be true, odds are it is.

Remember, the only people who truly benefit from these services are the ones who offer them and take your money in exchange for information that can easily be found on your own. Even many websites focused on the area of real estate investing are making money from affiliate links and by selling information that can be found for free elsewhere. In most cases, you will do just as well or better if you spend your own time and resources in gathering information and conducting research.

Supposed real estate gurus are in the market to sell you their ideas and hook you into investing. They aren't concerned with teaching you about the ins and outs of real estate investing at all. Instead, you need to rely on information, such as this guide, that provides the insights you need without costing additional money. You don't have to spend thousands of dollars on any training if you want to get started with your investments.

If you feel you would truly benefit from the help of a real estate investment professional, do your own research into their background and look for online reviews on third-party websites. This information will ensure you make a smart choice and aren't pulled in by a scammer. As long as you don't get caught up in empty promises of big bucks, you can find the assistance you need to make real estate investing a lucrative opportunity for your future.

Getting Started with No Cash, Really?

It may seem you would need some cash to invest in real estate. After all, you can't make a real estate transaction without it. Where that money comes from is the difference. You don't have to have any money of your own to get started in real estate investing, but you do need to find a

source of funding. However, when you intend to invest with other people's money, it's critical to learn how to market yourself and give others the confidence you can help them make money too.

If you don't have money of your own to invest and you want to pitch your idea to other investors, you need to determine what you can bring to the table. Perhaps you have a background in real estate or have the necessary connections to make smart real estate transactions. Maybe you have the time to spend on searching for the right properties at the lowest prices. Whatever you have to offer, you need to convince your backers to trust you with their money.

When you don't have your own money to bring to the table, you will need to find funding through other sources, such as:

- Partnerships;

- Low down payment loans;

- VA or no down payment loans;

- Wholesaling;

- Lease option strategies;

- Buying directly from sellers;

- Private funding; and

- Home equity loans or other lines of credit.

We will discuss each of these options a bit later in this real estate investing guide. The important thing to note here is yes, you can invest in real estate without having the money to fund it yourself. However, it isn't always an easy road. It takes diligence and creative thinking, as well

How Do You Earn Money in Real Estate without Investing

Investing isn't the only way to make money in real estate. If you either can't get the funds to start investing or you want to take a different approach, there are many lucrative career opportunities in the field. Among them include:

1. Mortgage Brokers;

2. Real Estate Agents/Brokers;

3. Real Estate Assistants;

4. Resident Managers;

5. Property Managers;

6. Appraisers, and

7. Title/Escrow Agents.

Starting in one of these career fields can be an excellent option to network and prepare for the world of real estate investing. You will gain valuable experience that will be an asset when you are ready to begin your investment ventures.

Real Estate Investing is Not a Get Rich Quick Scheme

You've likely seen advertisements showcasing a real estate professional living the good life while watching the money roll in from their investments. The truth is this isn't likely to happen, at least not until after long hours and years of dedication and a lot of financing. While there are some people who are wildly successful quickly, most people who take up real estate investing experience a slow climb to the top, if they reach it at all.

Investing in real estate is much like nurturing a young child or a new plant. It takes time, patience, planning and persistence if you want to be a success. You won't generate millions or even thousands of dollars in income within the first year or two, but you should see a steady increase over the years. It's important to focus on creating a solid foundation for a business that can grow into the future. Making money in real estate requires a lot of hard work, just like any other job you may have. There are no legitimate shortcuts that will allow you to make a lot of money fast and easy. However, once you learn the basics, you will have a good chance of generating the level of income you want, and potentially exceeding it.

Final Takeaway About Our Beginning

After reading this chapter, you should have a solid understanding of what is involved in real estate investing and whether it is a good fit for you. It doesn't matter if you think it is a good option for supplemental income or you choose to get involved on a full-time basis; real estate investing can be a lucrative method of creating a solid financial foundation for your family. The following chapters will delve more deeply into the process and give you valuable information you can use to make the most of your real estate investment venture.

2

EDUCATING YOURSELF IN REAL ESTATE

Without a solid understanding of the principles behind real estate investing, you increase your risks of failure. This is one of the most important chapters because it contains the background information you need to move forward with this type of financial venture. In this chapter, we will cover all of the real estate education you need to prepare yourself to get started.

There are Five (5) Distinct Ways to Make Money with Investment Property

Most people don't realize that there are five distinct ways to make money with investment properties. 1) Rental income paid by tenants which can go up over time as rents rise; 2) Property appreciation over time which will depend on location, inflation, etc.; 3) Tax benefits using depreciation will usually allow a completely tax-sheltered income stream; 4) Mortgage debt is being retired by other people's money; and 5) Mortgage payments at year one are not the same as they are at year 10, thus the future value of the same mortgage payment is cheaper than it was at year one.

Real Estate Investing Is All About Simple Math

You don't have to be a mathematical genius when it comes to real estate investing. In fact, much of the math you will need to do is simple addition, subtraction and multiplication. These basic formulas will show you the simplicity of real estate math to set your mind at ease.

- Income – Income or gross income is the amount of money you bring in from a particular property. This is probably the easiest equation of all the ones you will use. All you need to do is add the cost of the rent and any fees your tenants may pay. Some of the fees that can contribute to your income include parking fees, pet fees, late fees, laundry use and others.

- Expenses – After you figure your income from a property, you need to subtract the costs. First, you need to add up all the expenses, including your mortgage, garbage or other utility bills,

maintenance costs, and more. In addition to your monthly costs, make sure you consider other annual or bi-annual expenses, such as property taxes, insurance and others.

- Cash Flow – Once you have figured the income and expenses, you will be able to calculate your overall cash flow. This is another simple math equation. All you need to do is subtract the costs from the income you generate. The remainder represents your cash flow.

Calculating Your Return on Investment

Lenders collect an interest rate on the loans they offer because this is how they make money. In the real estate business, this is referred to as your return on investment. It refers to the amount of money you make back from what you put into a property. The calculation for this number is more complex than the others but still involves simple math you can easily do with the help of a calculator.

Simple Cash-on-Cash Rate of Return

Cash-on-cash return is a simple rate of return used in real estate transactions that calculates the cash income earned on the cash invested in an investment property. For example, when an investor purchases a rental property, they may put down only 10% for a cash down payment. Cash-on-cash return measures the annual return the investor made on the property in relation to the 10% down payment only. It provides a quick way for an investor to analyze an investment in real simple terms.

Leveraged Rate of Return

Leveraged return is a more complex rate of return used in real estate transactions that calculates the cash income earned on the cash plus loan invested in an investment property. This number provides a more complete way for an investor to analyze an investment in more complex terms.

Don't Miss This Step

Some individuals think they can skip out on the education aspect of real estate investing because they either think they know everything or they find it unimportant. Real estate investing is not a get rich quick scheme, which means you need to put some work and time into it before you see the returns you need. While this guide doesn't provide everything you need, it will give you the solid foundation you need to make the best decisions.

There are many options you can use to get the information you need to become a savvy real estate investor. The good news is you don't have to spend hundreds or thousands of dollars to get it. Below, we have compiled a list of potential resources that can help guide you through the process. Be sure to check them all out so you can find what works best for you.

- **Podcasts** – One of the newest methods of educating real estate investors, podcasts are audio recordings designed to provide information to listeners. There are a number of great real estate podcasts that can be streamed on computers, mobile devices, and even MP3 players so you can listen anywhere, any time. These podcasts cover a vast array of topics.

- **Blogs** – Blogging has become an important element of content marketing for all industries. In the real estate business, these blogs can be a great resource for those who are interested in investing. If you search for real estate blogs, you will find a large number of industry-relevant blogs that cover a variety of topics to help you gain a better understanding of the field.

- **Books** – While most people turn to the Internet for information first and foremost, books can still be a valuable resource. Head to your local library and check out the latest real estate investment books. Here, you will find books on every topic you can imagine relating to real estate and how to invest in it. You may also be able to find books on your e-reader or even download an audio book onto your smartphone or MP3 player.

- **Mentors** – Finally, you should look for someone else who is already involved in real estate investing to learn from firsthand experiences. There are a lot of professional investors who charge a premium for their help, but there are many more people who are willing to help for a fraction of the price. Start by introducing yourself to local real estate investors you wish to emulate. They will help you understand the local market and you will set yourself up with a potential partner for future investment opportunities.

Using Mentors to Help You Navigate the Process is Important

Mentors are those who have experience in a particular area and can help teach new individuals how to proceed. In the real estate investment arena, finding someone who can serve as your mentor is an invaluable resource. This individual can answer your questions, help you network, and show you what you should do to ensure your own success.

Think About Mentors in Your Life

Everyone has natural mentors in their lives. Think about the people who have had the biggest impact on your life. Parents, grandparents, bosses, teachers, siblings and others have served in the mentor role at some point in your life. The common thread between these individuals is it first started as a personal relationship and naturally evolved into a mentorship. You didn't reach an agreement; it just happened.

LinkedIn, Google+ or Other Online Groups May Be Helpful

LinkedIn & Google+ both have many investment groups – all of which provide decent investment advice and opportunities. If you don't have a LinkedIn or Google+ account, get one today and start looking and the real estate investing groups and join the ones that interest you and start reading the posts by the members. You will find that you will quickly start picking up the language, the opportunities, and some contacts.

Tips for Naturally Finding a Real Estate Investment Mentor

The great news is you don't have to spend thousands of dollars finding a high-end mentor. Organic mentors, which are those you find naturally, are people you can build a friendship with that will eventually transform into a mentor role.

You may wonder why an experienced real estate investor would take the time to help someone

who is just starting out. There are many reasons they may be eager to help. They may want to:

- Pass on their legacy to someone else;
- Find someone with similar interests to talk to; or
- Make potential deals.

This type of mentorship happens often under the guise of friendships. However, there is another side to this element. There are new real estate investors who feel mentors should want to work with them. They often boast online about looking for a mentor to teach them everything about investing in real estate, offering nothing in return. The fact remains the best mentorships are those where both parties contribute and strive to help each other in any way they can. In most cases, it's best to approach your search for a mentor through other means.

First and foremost, you need to find experienced investors you would like to learn from so you can begin building a friendship. You don't need a high-profile mentor to be successful. Instead, you can have success with someone who owns a few properties down the street from your home or an active member of a local real estate investment forum. The most important factor is finding someone who invests in the types of properties

you are interested in. For instance, if you are interested in investing in a multi-family apartment complex, you don't want someone who flips houses for a living. You need to find someone who is doing exactly what you want to do.

Next, you need to find something of value you can offer the other person. You may not know a lot about real estate investments, but there must be something they need. It could be something as simple as offering a few free hours to clean vacant apartments so they are ready to rent or contacting prospective renters. Perhaps you know a little about website design. Performing these services for free can be a great ice breaker, but depending on what you can offer, you may be able to expect some monetary compensation. For example, if you can perform basic maintenance services, you can charge a small fee for your services and save your mentor money on repairs that need to be made.

Above all else, do the above because you want to help, not because you expect something in return. Even though your mentor may be leagues ahead of you, that doesn't mean you can't provide some value to them that will help them be even more successful. When you give with no expectation to receive, your mentor will be more willing to help.

Most investors are willing to help others get started, but they want to make sure you are worthy of the assistance. A mentor isn't interested in wasting their time on someone who isn't serious about being successful. Mentoring someone takes a lot of time and effort, something they often cannot afford to waste. When you take the time to build your knowledge and show your persistence and your willingness to work toward your goals, you will earn the trust of your mentor.

You Should Never Pay for Mentorship

Having a mentor will help you grow your real estate investment business more quickly and easily than working on your own. Because it can take time to find a mentor organically, you may be tempted to pay for one. However, this isn't typically the best option.

There is so much information available online (i.e., LinkedIn mentioned above), much of it available at no cost, which means you should never have to pay to be taught how to get involved with real estate investing. There are also many forums and groups available that are available where you can ask questions and get answers from experienced investors.

While we don't find it necessary to pay for mentorship services, the choice is solely yours. Before you make a decision, check into whether their program is designed to make the process easier, but not necessarily shorter. You need to look at what you will spend on the program and what you are likely to make when you are done. The problem is most people are looking for a fast, easy way to get rich. Unfortunately, even paying for a mentorship won't produce results if you aren't willing to work for it.

Before you pay for training, it's important to look at the available resources to ensure you can't find the information you want for free, including looking for a free local mentor. Not only will this save you money, but it will make sure you are working with someone who understands the intricacies of the local market. If you still can't find a local mentor, you may be able to find the information you need from forums, books, blogs and other resources. This process will help you gauge your overall level of interest before you spend hundreds or thousands of dollars.

In addition, you need to determine which type of real estate investing you want to get involved in. Only then should you even consider paying for a mentorship of any kind. Before you settle on a paid mentorship, check them out with the Better Business Bureau and other reliable resources. Be wary of any glowing reviews found on websites designed to defend a company against bad reviews. You should also be aware of websites created to recycle information that can be found on numerous other websites. Do your research to ensure you avoid these scams.

Finally, don't be rushed into paying for a mentorship. Oftentimes, pitches are designed to appeal to the emotions of potential investors, urging them to act now. This high-pressure tactic is often a red flag. Don't be pressured into paying because you are afraid the deal will no longer be available or you are excited to get started.

Think about things for a few weeks and do some research. If you still feel it is a good choice, you can act on it.

One advantage of paying for mentors is it creates an additional layer of accountability. After all, you have spent hundreds or thousands of dollars on training, so you don't want to fail. Many investors have found success using paid mentors. However, success isn't guaranteed. Focusing on finding a free local mentor can prevent you from spending money on something that isn't guaranteed to work. Remember having a mentor isn't like buying a product or services; you will still need to do the work. Instead, working with a mentor can help guide you through the process so you can achieve your goals.

Fear Can Be Your Worst Enemy

If you look at all the successful real estate investors out there, you can feel confident there are dozens of others who were too afraid to even try. Fear and uncertainty are a normal part of the

Fear and uncertainty are a normal part of the process, but it can be your worst enemy, stopping you from reaching toward your goals.

process, but it can be your worst enemy, stopping you from reaching toward your goals.

Don't let fear stop you from getting started on the road toward a lucrative real estate investment career. The following is a list of steps you can take to help you overcome your fears and take that important next step.

1. Take Control. If you want your real estate investments to fully replace your current income, you will need to work hard for it and plan on many years to fully see the rewards. Create a plan to help you achieve your goals and start working on it every day. Successful real estate investors work hard every day, just as you get up and go to work every day. This won't be a fast or easy process, but the hard work will pay off, allowing you to work for yourself instead of continuing in a job you don't enjoy.

2. Make a Commitment. You have to be fully committed to taking control of your future in real estate investing before you start spending time and money on training and mentorships. No amount of training or research will do you any good if you aren't willing to put the work into it. When you are committed and focused on making real estate investing a part of your financial future, you can achieve success regardless of the techniques you use.

3. Get Involved. You don't have to be a passive member of the real estate investing world. Get involved by signing up for forums and attending conferences. The more you put your name out there, the more likely you will be to find an organic mentor or learn more about what you need to be successful. It also creates more visibility so people will begin to recognize you.

4. Talk the Talk. If you don't know the common terms used by those in the real estate investment field, you may feel behind or like you aren't sure what you are really talking about. Taking the time to learn the lingo will increase your level of confidence so you can boldly discuss real estate investing with anyone, especially others involved in the field.

5. Know the Concepts. After learning to talk the talk, you can move on to grasping the concepts used in the field. If you don't understand what an ARV is or what debt-to-income ratio means, you won't be able to explain it to anyone else either. When you don't understand common concepts used in real estate investing, your fear of the unknown can cause you to give up or make mistakes. Once you understand the concepts, try teaching them to someone else. Teaching can help cement these approaches in your mind.

6. Keep an Eye on Others. Spending time with others who are involved in the same type of real estate investing as you are can provide valuable insight into what makes them successful so you can replicate their practices. You may have to put in additional time and effort, but it will pay off in the end. When you see other investors are just like you and were able to succeed, you will feel more confident in your own level of success.

There is always some level of risk when it comes to any type of investment. Even though you can't entirely avoid taking risks, you can better manage them through the right research. Getting started is often the most difficult step. Don't let fear get in the way; just put yourself out there and start learning.

Many people to become trapped in what is known as "analysis paralysis." This term refers to the act of conducting research and building knowledge without ever taking actionable steps.

Don't Be Paralyzed in Analytics – Over Analysis Paralysis

Research and education are important elements in creating a successful real estate investment company of your own. However, it is easy for many people to become trapped in what is known as "analysis paralysis." This term refers to the act of conducting research and building knowledge without ever taking actionable steps. In most cases, this is caused by a fear of making a mistake when taking the first step.

Most people feel they need to know everything before they get started, which leads to more research and more time wasted. The fact is you don't need to know it all to get started. Much of it can be learned along the way. As long as you have enough information to focus on one area of investing, you can work on building up to others as you become more comfortable. Trying to take on too much at one time can lead to failure. We will cover the various niches you may want to consider later on in this guide.

After you determine the best starting point, you can work toward learning that niche more thoroughly. Real estate investment forums can be an excellent place to ask questions and share information. It will seem overwhelming to dive in before you truly feel ready, but the only way to overcome this feeling is to get your feet wet and start working. The fear will never go away until you take action. Getting involved will help you answer questions you have and even discover new inquiries you need answers to.

Fear can lead to spending more money or wasting your time on training you don't need. Repeating this process won't produce the results you're looking for. Instead, it's best to seek out the information you need, find a mentor, and dive right in so you can start working toward a more lucrative real estate investment career. Once you get started, you will experience an increase in confidence.

Moving Forward We Go

Now that you understand the depth of information you need to get started on this career path, you can move forward to the next step in this journey. In the next chapter, we will discuss more in-depth information you need to know to help you get started, such as the various real estate niches you may consider and the strategies you can use to achieve success. Armed with this information, you can move toward your career goals.

3

NICHES AND STRATEGIES FOR REAL ESTATE INVESTMENT

You may think you need to know absolutely everything about real estate investing before you get started, but the truth is you can focus on a smaller aspect first before building on your expertise. In this chapter, we will address some of the most popular niches and strategies so you can determine the best method of moving forward with your investments.

You Never Know What You're Going to Get

If you've ever encountered a box of chocolates in your life, you know there are so many choices it can be difficult to determine exactly what you want. The same is true when it comes to real estate investing. You may need to sample a few things before you find exactly what you like.

As you think about the real estate investing field, there may be areas or strategies you know without a doubt don't interest you. However, among those you aren't sure of, you will be able to find a clear picture of what each one offers and whether it would be a good fit for your end goals. If you want to be successful in the real estate investment field, you need to find a niche and strategy you want to approach and focus on that until you learn it well before expanding. Once you know exactly which niche you want to enter, you will be able to narrow your focus down even further so you don't become overwhelmed by the entire process.

You may think you need to know absolutely everything about real estate investing before you get started, but the truth is you can focus on a smaller aspect first before building on your expertise. In this chapter, we will address some of the most popular niches and strategies so you can determine the best method of moving forward with your investments.

You Never Know What You're Going to Get

If you've ever encountered a box of chocolates in your life, you know there are so many choices it can be difficult to determine exactly what you want. The same is true when it comes to real estate investing. You may need to sample a few things before you find exactly what you like.

As you think about the real estate investing field, there may be areas or strategies you know without a doubt don't interest you. However, among

those you aren't sure of, you will be able to find a clear picture of what each one offers and whether it would be a good fit for your end goals. If you want to be successful in the real estate investment field, you need to find a niche and strategy you want to approach and focus on that until you learn it well before expanding. Once you know exactly which niche you want to enter, you will be able to narrow your focus down even further so you don't become overwhelmed by the entire process.

Choosing Your Niche is a Process

There are many property types from which you can choose when you're selecting the ideal niche. Among these types of properties are many subsets. This is a brief overview of the areas in which you may want to get involved.

Empty Lot or Vacant Land?
What's the Difference

Not everyone is looking for a prebuilt home in which to move. This makes vacant or empty land in the right locations highly desirable. While it may seem that land is land, you can actually make improvements that will increase its value and make it more attractive to potential buyers. If you buy a large enough plot, you may be able to divide it into smaller pieces to sell for a profit. In some cases, the land may become more valuable over time based on other development in the area or its desirable location. It is critical to understand the zoning and planning regulations in that particular jurisdiction is before making any offers. Some lots already have the utilities available at the street adjacent to the parcel you are interested in. Other lots have utilities several hundred yards away – the cost to bring to your lot could be a deal breaker. Look-

ing and analyzing the title report, the zoning, the planning issues, and practical realities of building on a particular lot are all questions that need to be answered before you move forward with a lot purchase.

Single-Family Homes are Highly Desirable

Perhaps the most in-demand area of real estate, single-family homes are easy to rent out. Financing is also relatively straightforward and it's often easy to sell, especially after renovations. However, it's important to do your research and determine if the amount of rent you would receive will result in a positive cash flow. In some areas, the price of a rental doesn't meet the amount you would need to make a mortgage payment. Moreover, understand that with depreciation and proper tax planning a rental property that is not – on its face - breakeven may actually be so after taxes are calculated.

Small Multi-Family Properties May Provide Cash Flow Even with Vacancies

You don't have to invest in a large apartment building to take advantage of a multi-family income flow. These properties typically include duplexes, triplexes and fourplexes that house

between two and four families in one building. Because these homes are not as desirable as single family homes for those who are looking for a primary residence, it is often easier to purchase these properties for a low enough price to keep an adequate cash flow to stay in the positive. For some investors, these properties can also provide a primary residence, while still bringing in an income. The good news is you will only need one loan to secure this type of property, making it easier to invest bigger, especially if you are just starting out. These loans also often use the same guidelines as lending for single-family homes, making it much easier to obtain the funding you need to get started. Importantly, if you have one unit vacant it may still allow the property to breakeven or even cash flow positive.

Small Apartment Complexes are for More Experienced Investors

A small apartment complex is categorized as one that houses between five and 50 families. However, the difference between small and large apartments can be blurred. These complexes can often be more difficult to finance because they use the commercial standards for lending. This type of property is the perfect option for investors who don't mind the more intensive management tasks. Smaller apartment complexes often have less competition because they are too small for larger property management firms and too large for newer investors to be interested in.

When it comes to these properties, lenders consider the amount of income these properties bring in, rather than the actual value of the property. Because of this, you can improve the value of your property by increasing the amount of rent you charge and finding ways to reduce your expenses. Using onsite management to

perform maintenance and other management duties in exchange for free or reduced rent can be a great option for these complexes. Again a few vacancies will not necessarily ruin the cash flow.

Larger Apartment Buildings Usually Require On-Site Management

Most large apartment complexes include a number of amenities for their residents, including pools and fitness rooms. They often hire a full-time staff and have a large budget for advertising to help keep all of the units full with happy tenants. Because these properties often run in the multi-millions, they are often out of reach for smaller investors. For this reason, many of them are owned by larger property management firms, REITS, or syndications, which are groups of small investors who pool their money together to make a larger investment.

Real Estate Investment Trusts – A Creative Way to Invest in Real Estate

A Real Estate Investment Trust, or REIT, is similar to the difference between a mutual fund and a stock. Mutual funds are a group of stocks that are grouped together and sold to investors. Likewise, a group of smaller investors may pool their money together to invest in larger properties, such as shopping malls, skyscrapers, large apartment complexes, commercial buildings, and more. The manager of the REIT is then responsible for making sure each investor gets the appropriate share of any money made. This method of investing in real estate requires little knowledge and typically requires no input from individual investors. All you need to do is buy shares in the REIT and collect your earnings.

Commercial Buildings – Type A, B, C

Investing in a commercial building isn't often at the top of the list when people consider making a real estate investment, but they can be a lucrative option. This is one of the most versatile of real estate investment opportunities because of the variety of commercial real estate available. First and foremost, you need to decide if you want to rent smaller spaces to small, local businesses or you would rather target larger stores and national chains. One of the benefits of investing in commercial real estate is the cash flow is good as long as you can keep the property filled. However, these buildings often go through long periods of vacancy, which can end up costing you a lot of money. Therefore, it's important to wait until you have a solid financial foundation before investing in this type of real estate. Benefits of commercial buildings also usually include a robust expense reimbursement factors. Many commercial tenants sign triple-net leases wherein the tenants pay for all of the improvements of the property including structural components, roofing, plumbing, heating and air conditioning, insurance, common area maintenance and property taxes. Yes that's right, in triple-net leases the tenants pay for all of these expenses. Finally, Type A high-rise buildings are the premier investment grade, Type B is a lower quality, and Type C is the lowest quality of commercial investment grade buildings.

Tax Liens as an Investment Strategy

Not all homeowners are able to keep up with the expenses of owning a home. When taxes go unpaid, the government can foreclose on a home, even if the mortgage is up-to-date. Reselling the property helps them gain back the money lost and gives investors a great opportunity to buy a property for less. However, extensive research is necessary before getting involved in this type of investment because they are often complicated transactions that require some level of expertise to navigate successfully.

Notes – Not Your Grade School Type

Notes are probably one of the least recognizable of the investment types available to you. A note

is defined as the contract explaining the terms of the loan. In most cases, these notes aren't completed through a bank. Instead, the owner of a building may agree to carry the full note of the purchase price and the buyer agrees to pay a certain amount plus an interest rate over a specified period of time.

Sometimes an owner decides they no longer want the responsibility of the note and may choose to sell it to another investor or group of investors instead. In most cases, this note will be sold at a reduced amount than what is owed. The note can be completed by the note buyer or it can be resold again in the future.

Property Niche Summary

The above described niches which you may choose to invest in, along with some of the pros and cons of each type of investment provide a broad foundation of opportunity. In general, it is best to start with one and learn it well before moving on to add another. The good news is there are many options to choose from if your first selection doesn't work out.

After you have selected your preferred niche, you will need to move onto finding a strategy that works best. The next section will address the various strategies investors can use and which niches they each work best in.

Which Real Estate Investment Strategy Is Best for You

Choosing a niche isn't the only decision you have to make. You also need to research and explore the various investment strategies that exist so you can make the smartest choice. In many cases, you will need to combine multiple

strategies to ensure the best results. Below, we will explore three of the most common investment strategies. However, keep in mind this is a brief overview and more extensive research may be required.

Buy & Hold Strategy – A Marathon

This is the most common method of investing in real property, especially when it comes to residential properties. In simple terms, it refers to buying the property and renting it out for a profit. Some investors see it as an opportunity to generate a passive flow of income by continuing to rent the property out, while others rent it out with the intention of selling it when the market is favorable to a profit. One of the biggest reasons investors choose this strategy is because the rent charged is often enough to keep the mortgage paid, which reduces the principle and increases the amount of equity you have when it's time to sell.

Before you move forward with this strategy, you need to recognize how to identify which deals and opportunities are the best options. If you don't fully understand property valuation and average rent in your area, it's easy to make a bad deal that will cost you money, rather than making a profit. Some of the other common issues new investors encounter with this strategy include:

- Underestimating Expenses

- Choosing the Wrong Tenants

- Poor Property Management

Learning the business of real estate investing and property management can help you avoid all of these problems and increase the chances of a successful investment experience.

In order to succeed in this type of property investment strategy, you need to know how to evaluate the fluctuations in the real estate market of your target area. Like any other type of investment, it is ideal to buy when prices are low. As the market turns, investors may consider selling properties or continue to hold onto them for a passive income. Some investors never choose to sell their properties, despite changes in the market, but would rather use it as a source of income for the long-term.

The buy and hold process may seem like a straightforward strategy, but there is so much more to it than at first glance. However, if you take the time to learn how to find the best deals, locate ideal tenants and take care of the property, there is a good chance you will see success with this investing strategy.

Flipping Homes - Fixers

You've probably seen television shows where individuals buy run down homes for a low price and spend weeks or months renovating the property into a beautiful home that sells for far more than the original purchase price. This strategy takes advantage of the principle of buying low and selling high.

Most investors work with single-family homes when it comes to flipping properties. This is primarily due to the ease of obtaining financing and the minimal amount of work most homes need. Most investors follow a percentage rule, which states they buy homes for a 'certain' percent of the value minus the renovation costs to ensure a positive return. However, it's important to remember this is a rule of thumb and your actual numbers may vary depending on where the property is located.

One of the biggest factors you need to consider is the speed at which you can flip the home. The faster you can complete the work and sell, the less money you will lose paying the bills, which may include:

- Loan Payments

- Utility Bills

- Insurance

- Property Taxes

- Maintenance Bills

- HOA Fees

Another thing to remember is flipping homes isn't a passive activity. There is a lot of work involved and you need to keep going if you want to make a living doing this. After you sell one home, you need to buy another and flip that one to ensure a steady flow of income. This practice can be used to pay your household bills, as well as fund other passive investments in the future.

Wholesale Real Estate

The wholesale real estate market isn't one most people think of when they think of real estate investing. During this process, investors look for a great deal and sign the contract to make the purchase. Before that purchase is completed, they then sell the contract to someone else with an added assignment fee. This fee ensures a small profit for your work. The good news is you will never actually own the property because you serve as a middle man facilitating the purchase.

While some of these wholesale investors sell to retail clients, others make it their priority to sell to other investors who many not have the time or expertise to find the best deals. Many of these investors pay in cash, which allows wholesalers to get paid quickly.

Despite the fact this method of investing isn't as well known, it can be one of the easiest to start with because there are few costs. Because the investor never takes actual possession of the property, there are no fees, loans, rehab costs, tenant issues or anything else most real estate investors encounter.

If this is the type of real estate investing that appeals most to you, it's important to always be on the lookout for great real estate deals. It's also critical to maintain a well-organized sales funnel so you always have investors at the right stage in the buying process so you can unload your inventory as quickly as possible. While this is something anyone can do because it requires no financial commitment, you need to work hard to make sure you have buyers ready to purchase the contracts. This may require a financial investment in building a sales funnel, which may include content marketing and other forms of advertisement. With the right dedication and hard work, this can be a lucrative option for your investments.

Final Thoughts

The information found in this chapter can help you more effectively grasp the different types of investments you can make, as well as the strategies you can use to produce the results you want. You may still be unsure of what direction you would like to take, but you have a good start on research to help guide you in the right direction. You may be excited about getting involved at this point, but there is still more to learn—particularly, how to write an effective business plan so you can make the right choices.

If you want to be successful in the real estate investment field, you need to find a niche and strategy you want to approach and focus on that until you learn it well before expanding.

4

CREATING AN EFFECTIVE BUSINESS PLAN

Going into real estate investing without a plan is a recipe for disaster. Before you get started in the investment field, it's important to create a plan you can follow to ensure your success. In this chapter, we will help guide you through the process of putting together your own plan to improve your chances of a successful real estate investment venture.

Writing Your Plan – Plan to Succeed

Most people don't drive through unfamiliar territory without a map or a GPS because it tells you where to go without getting lost and wasting time. Maps and GPS devices show you the easiest way to get from one place to another. The same is true of your business

plan. It will serve as your road map to help you achieve your goals in the real estate investment market.

What Should Your Business Plan Include

When you first look at a business plan, it can be overwhelming. You may wonder how you will be able to put one together without forgetting something. The following tips will help guide you through the steps to ensure you don't miss any important details.

■ Mission Statement – Your mission statement should tell people your purpose in real estate investment. Why are you interested in real estate investments? Do your research so you

can more effectively portray your reasons behind your plans.

- Goals – While some people confuse the mission statement and goals or feel they are interchangeable, they are indeed different. A goal is what you want to accomplish through your real estate investments. This can be the number of homes you wish to purchase and re-sell or how much income you would like to make per month. Be sure to address both short-term and long-term goals and adjust them as needed.

- Strategy – There are so many ways you can make money in real estate. Therefore, this section should address exactly how you plan to approach this task. Do you want to buy and flip homes to build a fast cash flow? Maybe you want to generate a passive income you can rely on into your retirement years. It's okay if you don't know how you plan to accomplish all of your goals. Your business plan isn't static and will need to be adjusted over time.

- Timeline – How long will it take you to reach your goals? This is the place for all of your other time-related elements, such as when you would like to retire or when you want to quit your regular job, if those are your goals. This is the place to document your timeline so you can track your success.

- Market – Who are you trying to reach? Do you want to look for properties in low-income areas or perhaps you want to specialize in commercial buildings? Most new investors plan to keep their investments close to home where they can keep a close eye on them. Once they gain more experience, they can expand their reach. Focusing on a smaller area will help you learn more and so you can grow and increase your income. For example, properties in other states may provide better cap rates and cash-on-cash returns.

- Criteria – You won't want to purchase every home or business building that crosses your path. This is the area of your business plan where you will detail just what you are looking for in an investment. Do you want to invest primarily in single-family homes or are you interested in a long-term apartment building investment? What are the must-haves in a home and how much are you willing to spend? The most important thing to remember is to set realistic criteria and stick to it.

• Flexibility – After your initial business plan is complete, you may find the criteria you set or the strategy you chose isn't producing the results you want, you will need to make adjustments.

• Marketing Plan – As a real estate investor, you need to find ways to attract sellers to you—or, in other words, a solid marketing plan. You also need to find ways to locate the best deals. What avenues will you use to locate these deals? We will discuss marketing strategies in a later chapter.

• Financing – This area of your business plan requires you to think about how you will obtain the financing for the deals you make. Do you have the funds yourself to pay for these deals or do you need to obtain financing from banks, private lenders or other investors? This is often one of the biggest challenges for investors today. If you can find the best ways to attract private funding,

this is often one of the easiest solutions to this problem.

• Deal Handling – How you will handle your deals is another important element in your business plan. You need to make sure you clearly define the steps you will take to achieve your goals and land the deals you want. It's also important to make sure you have a list of exit strategies to help you get out of deals that go bad. It's important to have a top-notch team in place including an experienced realtor, lender, inspector, and property manager to name a few.

• Teams and Systems – Who will you have working with you and what system do you plan to use to achieve your goals? You also need to consider whether you will need to hire an attorney or a CPA as part of your process. At this point of writing your business plan, you don't need to know who will fill these roles.

• The Backup Plan – Things don't always go smoothly in the world of real estate marketing. Therefore, it's important to make sure you have a backup plan and exit strategy to help you get out of the deals that aren't shaping up in your favor. In addition, you need to know how you intend to unload the properties, such as flipping and selling, renting or leasing the property or using any other technique.

• Provide Examples of the Deals – Potential financial backers want to know what you have in mind with the deals you intend to make. Showing people what you intend to do with your real estate investments can get them excited about it. You can address cash flow, funding, returns on investment and more. This area of your business plan is one of the most likely to change as your approach adjusts over time.

• Your Financial Status – This area of your business plan should talk about where you stand financially today. What do you bring to the deal and how can you benefit the other investors? They want to know if you are bringing in no financial support or if you have equity you can use to help back the deals. Keep this area updated as you move forward with your investments and your financial situation changes.

• A Final Note – It's important to realize your business plan should be treated as a guide, rather than a set-in-stone plan. It should motivate you to follow it, but it can be adjusted and changed with your needs. It's nearly impossible to follow your plan perfectly, but once you recognize its intent, you will feel more confident. There are many outside sources that can derail your plan. It's how you handle these challenges that will dictate whether you are a success. Stick to it as closely as you can and you will come out on the other side.

If you find people who have failed in real estate investing, you will find one of the biggest factors is a lack of preparation and dedication.

Putting Together Your Team

Investors often need to do a lot of the work themselves, but you may need some assistance along the way. The good news is you won't have to hire full-fledged employees to complete the work for you. Instead, it is a collection of individuals you can turn to for a number of services. The following are team members you should consider adding.

• A Mentor – If you want to be successful, you need someone who has been successful to help guide you through the process. When you work with someone who has already achieved similar goals to yours, it increases the chances you will be successful as well.

• A Loan Broker/Officer – If you don't have the cash to fund this venture on your own, you need someone who can help you get the funding you need to be successful. A mortgage broker can often be your best choice for helping you find the lowest rates. In addition, loan officers may also be able to help you find buyers and properties in which you can invest.

■ Attorney – Real estate investing requires a lot of contracts. Consider having a real estate attorney on hand to help you read through these contracts and understand the legalities of your investments. It can feel intimidating to spend the money to keep a lawyer on hand, but it can be an important component to a successful career. In some cases, you can put off paying fees until you close deals.

■ Title Rep or Escrow Officer – If you live in a state that uses an escrow officer or title rep, it's important to have one you work closely with. They can help you close the deals more quickly and feel confident they are looking out for your best interests.

■ Accountant – No matter how good you are at math and handling your personal finances, having an accountant on your team is a must. As you purchase more properties, handling your taxes becomes more difficult. Be sure you choose an accountant who understands the real estate field. They will help you under-

stand what you can write off and help you maximize your credits.

■ Insurance Agent – Whether you plan to flip and sell the properties or you will keep them and rent them out, you will need insurance on each one. Working with an insurance broker can help you search for the best deals and keep your costs low.

■ Contractor(s) – Even if you don't plan on flipping a home, having a contractor on your team is necessary because there will be repairs that need to be made. As a landlord, you need to be able to meet the needs of your tenants. Look for someone who will complete the work on time and under your budget.

■ Family and Friends Who Support You – Real estate investing is a time-consuming task. You will go further if you have family and friends who will support you through the process.

■ Realtor/Broker – Because you are buying and selling properties, it makes sense to find a real estate agent you can rely on to help you through the process. You or a family member may even wish to look into becoming a real estate agent so you have access to the tools you need. If you go with someone else, find someone who is

It's important to put together a team of professionals who can help you achieve the results you want.

dedicated and responsive. Because they are paid based on the sale price of the property, they are an excellent resource you can rely on to show you properties, hold open houses when you sell and more.

▪ Property Manager – If you are capable of managing your own properties, you don't need this piece of your team. However, if you will have many properties or would rather focus on other areas of your life, a property manager can make your life easier with more effective managing techniques.

▪ A Handyman/Day Porter – Little things will come up as tenants come and go through your properties. Having a handyman who can provide these services is essential to your success. Ask for referrals from other landlords in your area to find the best people at the job. Great handymen often have no need to advertise because they get plenty of business through referrals.

Referrals from other investors are the best way to build your team. In most cases, experienced investors are eager to share their expertise with other newer investors. Sharing their favorite referrals helps build professional relationships.

Building a Great Real Estate Team

It's important to put together a team of professionals who can help you achieve the results you want. It's difficult to put together a strong team, but with hard work and research, you can gather a variety of people to support you.

Investors who flip homes or those who have a lot of properties rely on their team more than those who are just starting out or only have one or two properties. If one member of your team doesn't do their job properly, it can negatively impact your results. You need to work with a team that strives to get results, not makes excuses for not getting the work done.

As you make your selections, be wary of people who talk overly positively about their skills. Instead, look at the results they achieve and the traits they exhibit. Having long conversations with potential contractors and other prospective members of your team will help you make the right choices. Some of the information you should look for include:

- Their expertise

- How they interact with you

- Their level of responsiveness

- Their ability to meet deadlines

- Clear and timely communication

It will take time to build your team and many of the members you won't need right way so take your time finding the right people. After you have built your team, you will be able to move toward meeting your goals.

Going Alone or Choosing a Partner

Not everyone decides to start the real estate investing journey on their own. Joining forces with someone else in a partnership can be helpful. However, this isn't a one-size-fits-all solution. You need to look at your financial resources, the amount of time you can commit and where your abilities lie. If you're considering a partnership, you need to look at the pros and cons, as well as what type of partnership you want to pursue.

The Pros of a Partnership

There are a number of pros to selecting someone to partner with, including:

- Brainstorming – There is some truth to the saying two heads are better than one. Someone else may be able to supplement your ideas with their own to build a stronger strategy.

- More Resources – A single person may have limited resources, but if you pool your resources with another investor, you can have a stable investing experience.

- Analytical Assistance – Analysis is an important part of a successful real estate investment venture. While you may be good at analyzing your numbers, sometimes someone else can give you additional insight into how well the business is doing.

- Complementary Strengths – Everyone has their different strengths and it's important to choose a partner who complements your own. Choosing someone who is just like you is often a bad decision. Look for someone who will bolster your weaknesses so you can increase your chances of success.

- Divide Tasks – Depending on how many investments you intend to make, handling it all can quickly become overwhelming. Partnering with someone else allows you to divide up the tasks based on what each person excels at and ensures everything gets done.

- More Networking – Networking is such an important part of the real estate investing world. In addition to having someone else who can help you with this task, your partners will likely come into your partnership with some connections of their own, which might be useful to you.

- Greater Confidence – Real estate investing can be overwhelming, especially for a new-comer. Working with someone else can help boost both of your confidence and provide the motivation you need to move forward.

- Reduce Your Risk – Because you aren't the only one who has a vested interest in the real estate you buy, you will reduce your risk of loss. Your partner will absorb some of the losses, just as you will both benefit when you succeed.

The Cons of a Partnership

Entering a partnership isn't the perfect option for everyone. Before you start looking for the ideal candidate, consider these negatives.

- Personality Issues – Not everyone gets along, which is a normal part of life. Because you will work so closely together and rely on each other for support, it's easy for personality conflicts to get in the way.

- Opinion Differences – In addition to potential personality conflicts, you may also encounter differing opinions on important issues. While some people can resolve these problems diplomatically, it can drive a rift between you that can quickly cause your business to buckle.

- Trust Issues – There is a lot of money involved in real estate investing. If you don't fully trust your partner, you could be facing serious problems. Trust often takes a long time to build and one minor thing can cause it all to come crumbling down. Fraud is a serious risk when you're working with a partner, especially if it's someone you don't know well.

- Slow Decisions – Some decisions in the real estate field need to be made quickly. However, when you're working with someone else who has equal input, it can sometimes take longer to make these critical choices, as well as any minor options.

- Reduced Profits – Lowering financial risks may be one of the benefits of choosing a partnership, but there is another side to the coin. You will also receive lower profits as well.

- Mixing Business with Pleasure – Whether you choose someone who was already a friend or

Responsibility

A duty or obligation upon one
moral, or legal accountability
to behave correctly in respec
ability or authority to act or
take decisions independentl

you feel yourself growing closer with your partner, it's rarely a good idea to mix friendships with your business dealings. While it's great to have the support of a friend, you can quickly spoil your friendship with bad business deals.

• Unrealistic Expectations – Most people know how they want things done and expect everyone else will do them the same. In a partnership, this isn't always the case. Remember, the other party has their own ideas how things should go. If your partner doesn't live up to your expectations, it can quickly lead to a failed partnership.

• Responsibilities – When you enter a partnership, you both have the same liabilities as the other party. In essence, a partnership is tying you both together. If someone makes a serious mistake, you will both be held liable for it. Be sure you ask your real estate attorney to write up an ironclad agreement to ensure nothing is left up to interpretation.

Tips for a Successful Partnership

Once you choose to enter a partnership on your real estate investment journey, there are a few tips you can follow to ensure a smoother journey:

- Compromise – In a partnership like this, there will be disagreements. Learn how to compromise to ensure you are both happy with the results.

- Plan Ahead – As you enter your new partnership, plan out who will handle what tasks, how you will handle disagreements and how profits will be split. The more you plan, the more smoothly it will go.

- Be Kind – No one wants to work with someone who is stubborn and doesn't treat them well. Be patient and treat your partner with the same level of respect you expect.

- Keep Communication Open – It's important to touch base with your partner on a daily basis. Always keep in touch about the state of daily goals and to discuss future plans with your investments.

The Bottom Line is

When it comes to partnerships, there are a lot of benefits, though they aren't the perfect fit for everyone. Even if you choose not to go with a partnership, you won't have to face the world of real estate investments on your own. There are plenty of other investors you can talk to about starting on your own and getting referrals from. You can also outsource many of the tasks you either don't have the time to complete or the skills to handle. While this will cost money, it saves you from having to share your profits right down the middle.

In California an "S" corporation or an LLC may be best suited for your enterprise as they are "pass-thru" tax entities, where the individual shareholders pay individual income tax on their income from the entity.

If you do choose to find a partner, take precautions from the start. It can be difficult to find someone you can trust enough to work with, but with the proper research and finding someone who shares the same goals and ideals as you, you will be able to create an effective plan that benefits both of you. As long as you are both committed to making things work, you will be able to achieve great things.

Structuring Your Business Entity

One of the most difficult aspects of starting a real estate investment business, regardless of whether it is a partnership or a solo venture, is how to structure it. It's important to protect yourself from personal liability, separating your personal finances from your business life. In most cases, it's best to work with a real estate attorney to go over the different options and determine which one best suits your situation. In California an "S" corporation or an LLC may be best suited for your enterprise as they are "pass-thru" tax entities, where the individual shareholders pay individual income tax on their income from the entity. A "C" corporation may be required for more complex organizations – which is a separate taxable entity. In either case a competent real estate attorney can help you through this decision process.

Final Thoughts

Just like a building, your real estate investment business needs a solid foundation in order to be structurally sound. In this chapter, you have learned how to create a strong business plan so you can focus on building the type of business you envision. After choosing a niche, you need to determine whether you want to work with someone or alone and then create a business plan to guide you through the entire process.

As you continue through this guide, we will go on to provide information regarding how you can find the ideal investment opportunities to maximize your returns.

5

LOCATING INVESTMENT PROPERTIES

The previous chapters have all discussed the preparations you need to make before you start your investment journey. Once you are ready to take the next step and look for properties to purchase, you need to think about how you will achieve the results you want. In this chapter, we will discuss what to look for, how to negotiate a good deal and give you tips for getting through the process, all the way through closing.

Making a Profit on Your Real Estate Investments

It may seem unusual, but the profit you make from your real estate investments essentially come when you purchase the property. You can't expect a large profit from the start of your investment journey. Instead, you need to implement successful investment strategies that help you buy properties for the lowest possible price and turn them around to sell for a higher price. Buy too high and you will find it negatively impacts your profit potential.

While it's impossible to predict what the future holds in terms of the housing or commercial real estate markets, you will gradually learn how to minimize your risks as time goes along and you gain experience.

An Example of Comparable Properties

Consider a home that is listed for sale at $140,000. Upon researching similar builds in the same area, you find they sold between $130,000 and $160,000. As you look more closely at the home you are considering, you may see it requires at least $20,000 worth of repairs, not including any of the other costs associated with buying or selling the home. If you aren't careful, you could find you owe more money on a home than it is worth, making it nearly impossible to turn a profit because the margin is too small. However, if similar homes are valued higher, you will be able to make money from your investment.

If you aren't going to be selling and want to keep the property as a rental, you need to implement similar analytic strategies. Look closely at the monthly expenses associated with owning the property and compare it to the average amount of rent received by other landlords who own properties in the area (for example or rents available see http://www.rentometer.com). If your monthly expenses surpass the money you can bring in, you may not be making a sound financial decision.

It's easy to count on an upswing in the market to help you make more money on your real estate investments, but you should never rely on appreciation, especially in today's market. The profit you make off a property depends solely on the amount of money you spend on said property today, not how much it may be worth. Trying to guess whether a value will rise puts you at risk, whether you're just starting out or you have invested in other properties before.

Set Your Criteria

Most people wouldn't go to the grocery store without at least a basic outline of the things they need. Keeping this example in mind, why would you start looking for investment properties without a list of what you want? Before you search for potential investments, you should put together a list of your criteria. This can stop you from being distracted by features that catch your eye but aren't on your carefully vetted catalog of must-

haves for your investments. You can always consider adding these new qualities at a later date.

While real estate is an exciting field, it can quickly become overwhelming for beginners. If you don't head into potential deals with a checklist of what a rental property should and shouldn't have, you may begin buying whatever properties come your way and are within your budgetary reach. Having an index in front of you can help you focus and keep you in the right direction. You will be able to quickly narrow down your choices and avoid unnecessary properties. With a list you can focus on exactly what you want.

Creating Your List and Checking it Twice

As you begin evaluating which criteria you want in an investment property, you need to consider the niche you want to enter as discussed in previous chapters. Crafting a concrete tally of criteria will help you narrow down your options. Some elements you may want to consider include:

- Neighborhoods, Location

- Towns, Cities, Localities

- Property Size, Bedrooms, Bathrooms

- Property Condition, Updated, Original

- Cap Rate Purchase Price

- Appreciation Potential

- Number of Units (Multi-Family)

The bottom line is the criteria for your investments are a widely personal choice. No one can give you an answer as to whether your choices are right or wrong. Much of it depends on what strategy you will be using. If you intend to hold

onto the property and rent it out, you should invest in something that is newer and requires little work. However, if you are going to flip the home, you may not want to be as selective because you intend to make improvements anyway.

When you create a list of requirements ahead of time, you will be able to more easily get through your search. You will also find it easier to tell your real estate agent exactly what you are looking for to further narrow down your choices. The more specific you are, the easier time your agent will have matching you with properties that can meet your needs and your budget.

Understanding the Rules of Engagement

Finances are the most difficult aspect of creating your criteria. In the end, you need to know whether a purchase is in your best interests or it will be a poor investment. We previously discussed some of the math surrounding investments. Now is the time to put it into practice. Unfortunately, a listing isn't going to provide all of the information you need to understand the financial status of a property. You may be able to determine the amount of income the property is capable of generating. However, you won't be able to precisely determine monthly cash flow, how much you should offer and whether they are asking too much. It's often far too time-consuming to complete a full financial analysis of every property you are considering. However, if you use these rules, you will be able to quickly assess the value of your potential investment and make a fast decision.

The Two Percent Rule

Some investors employ a 2% rule – in short the amount of rent you charge on a property should be two percent of the purchase price. However, this is just a baseline. It can help you determine how much you should bid on a home to ensure you get the most out of your investment. For instance, if the average rent of a three-bedroom home is $1,000, you shouldn't spend more than $50,000. Unfortunately, this rule is difficult to achieve in many locations, which means you need to put a little more thought into whether buying the property makes sound financial sense.

The 50 Percent Rule

Some investors utilize a 50% rule when analyzing potential investment property. A property's monthly expenses are another important element in determining the value of an investment - this rule states that about 50 percent of your income from the property will go toward monthly costs, such as insurance, vacancies, management costs, repairs and more. This amount does not include the mortgage payment. When you look at real estate listings, you should know the income the property generates each month. When you divide that number in half, you will see how much money you should have left after you pay the mortgage. Anything beyond your monthly expenses and the mortgage payment will become your positive cash flow.

It's important to realize all of the payments that go into owning and maintaining a rental property. This 50 percent rule is designed to help you properly budget and determine if the investment is financially sound. It also helps you plan for unexpected costs.

The 70 Percent Rule

The 70 percent rule is designed to make it fast and easy to determine how much you should be willing to bid on a home based on the after repair value (ARV). This rule is primarily used by house flippers because they want to sell properties quickly after purchasing them. This rule simply states you should never pay more than 70 percent of the value of the home after finishing repairs, minus the amount needed to complete said repairs.

Because this is only a rule of thumb, it's important to use it as one factor when evaluating

whether a property is worth considering. You should never use it to determine exactly how much you should bid, but it can give you a starting point. As long as a property passes this rule and the other rules of thumb, it can be a helpful benchmark when you are making a decision to purchase an investment property.

Where Can I Find Potential Investment Properties?

Once you are ready to start looking at properties, you need to know where to look. Driving around the neighborhood isn't the best choice to find properties for sale that fit your criteria. Below you will find a list of resources you can use to help you navigate the path of real estate investments.

▪ MLS – The Multiple Listing Service, or MLS, is used by real estate agents and brokers to help their clients find properties. This comes directly from a large number of properties listed for sale through various real estate agencies.

These are among the easiest to find when you search online.

▪ Newspaper – While not as widely used anymore, the local newspaper can still be a valuable resource (in some localities). Here you can find homes for sale by their owners, rather than through real estate agencies. Sometimes these individuals are willing to sell for less than they would through a real estate agent.

▪ Word of Mouth – Spread the word you are looking to invest in real estate and some investment opportunities may find their way to you. There are many places you can share this fact, including a local real estate club or among your own family and friends.

▪ Craigslist – While you should be cautious with Craigslist, it can be a valuable resource in your search for the perfect investments. There are millions of Craigslist users so you are bound to find an array of options from which you can choose.

• Outbound Marketing – For those who have money to spare, outbound marketing can be an excellent resource. You can use direct mailings, telemarketing calls, various advertising techniques and more to seek out properties you can invest in.

• LinkedIn.com Investor Groups – LinkedIn has many features, one of which is Groups. There are groups for just about every investment category including residential & commercial real estate. You will find investors who specialize in residential, commercial, smaller multi-family properties, larger apartment complexes, restaurants, shopping centers and much more, all available for the price of a little research and due diligence. If you don't already have a LinkedIn profile you should set one up right away and begin to look at all the opportunities available at your fingertips.

• Loopnet.com – For commercial properties, this website is the perfect option. You will find smaller multi-family properties, larger apartment complexes, restaurants, shopping centers and much more, all available through public listings. You will need to create an account – or hook up with a broker who has access to the site.

Buying Properties for Investment

After you have done your research and have found the right properties to buy, you can begin the buying process. Because the buying process is lengthy and complex, it's important to break it down in easy-to-follow steps for the best results.

• Step One: Determine your investment niche, your risk tolerance, and strategies as discussed in previous chapters.

• Step Two: Create a list of criteria you require before you invest; i.e., you want to look specifically at multi-family residential buildings.

• Step Three: Determine financing for your purchases. Having this clear plan in place will help you achieve your goals and ensure you have the funds you need. If you will be using a bank loan, make sure you get pre-approved. However, if you intend to use cash, make sure it's ready to go at the time of purchase. If you have other investors make sure they are ready, willing and able to move forward with their money – as you don't want to be 'left at the altar' when the perfect deal is presented to you.

• Step Four: Start looking for properties that match your criteria. Watch all of your resources (MLS, Listing Alert, Brokers, Craigslist, etc.), and put together a list of properties you would like to look at. This is also the time to contact a real estate agent or broker to help you in your search. However, if you'll be dealing with homes listed privately, you won't need an agent.

• Step Five: Once you have a list of potential properties, you need to run them through your checklist. This will ensure you aren't bidding on properties that don't meet your criteria.

• Step Six: Make offers on the properties you want. In many cases, it's best to start lower than you are willing to pay to leave room for negotiation. This helps the seller feel confident in getting more without going over your set budget. If you are using a real estate agent, they will have an offer form to fill out. However, if you are buying without the assistance of an agent, you may be able to find blank forms from a number of resources, including attorneys, title companies and even paper supply stores. It's important to run everything by an experience realtor, broker or real estate attorney before submitting the offer.

• Step Seven: Negotiate your deal with the seller. You may experience counter offers and go back and forth until you settle on a price and terms.

• Step Eight: Inspect the property thoroughly – and follow recommendations by the professional inspectors. Not only will you need a proper examination of the property you are buying, but you will also need to complete a lot of the other paperwork required to purchase it. This includes submitting all the necessary paperwork to complete your financing and preparing for the closing process. This step could take days, weeks or even months, depending on how easy it is to gather all the necessary documentation.

• Step Nine: Once the financing is in place, inspections are complete and you are ready to move forward with the process, you will meet with the title and escrow company and sign closing documents. The seller will also be signing all of their paperwork about the same time.

▪ Step Ten: Close escrow, take possession and begin your investment business.

Final Thoughts

At this point, you should have a solid understanding of how to set the criteria for your investments, including your personal and financial require-ments. Composing a detailed list will help you make the most reasonable decisions to protect your investments. You will quickly be able to weed out any properties that aren't the best option in favor of those that are most likely to be profitable. You should also have a firm understanding of the buying process and what that means for your investments.

In the next chapter, we will cover real estate financing, as well as the various methods that are available to help you achieve your investment goals.

6

FINANCING REAL ESTATE INVESTMENTS

There's no way to invest in the real estate market without funding. While most investors don't have the cash on hand to invest in real estate and pay 100% cash there are plenty of options available to help you get the funds you need to get started. We will explore these options and help you determine which one is right for you and your goals.

The Importance of Understanding Real Estate Financing

There is a variety of financing available for real estate, which is why we need to dig deeper into the topic. We previously discussed the different types of properties you can invest in, as well as the strategies you can use. However, we haven't yet talked about the various methods of financing and why it is necessary.

YOUR GUIDE TO REAL ESTATE INVESTING

This chapter will help you gain a better understanding of your financing options. While this isn't a comprehensive list, it will help you evaluate your financing choices and make a more informed decision. This chapter will help you put everything together so you can start moving forward with your investment strategy.

All Cash Investments Aren't Always What They Seem

Being able to pay for all of your investments with cash can be a great way to make money, but most people can't achieve this goal right off the bat. Only about a quarter of investors use their own cash to pay for real estate investments. It's important to understand no one brings actual cash to closing. Most investors will issue a cashier's check to the title company, which will then write a check to the seller. Wire transfers may be used to complete the transaction. One of the advantages of paying in cash is the absence of complications.

Paying all cash for a property might seem impressive, but it isn't necessarily the best use of your money in the long term. In fact, some savvy investors merely use an 'all cash' purchase to

obtain the property – as it is an attractive offer in a seller's eyes – but immediately refinance and take their cash out once the deal has closed escrow. The reason for this is that a smaller down payment will improve one's cash-on-cash return – taking full advantage of leverage. This strategy will free up the investor's cash reserves and allow them to purchase another property.

Conventional Mortgages Still Number One

Even if you have the cash, it may be wiser to use it as a down payment on multiple properties, with a traditional mortgage financing the rest. If you can afford to put 20 percent down, it can be useful to apply for a conventional mortgage for financing. These mortgages are the same as those used by traditional buyers and often have lower interest rates. If you have more to invest, you can increase your down payment to 25 to 30 percent instead.

Portfolio Lenders – Creative Approach

There are many sources for conventional loans, such as banks, credit unions and mortgage brokers. These lenders often get their capital from other sources, such as borrowing funds from another party or by selling the loan to another provider. For this reason, these lending institutions they must stick to strict rules and regulations. This can make it difficult to obtain a loan through traditional means.

In these situations, portfolio lenders can be a smart choice. Some credit unions and banks are capable of providing loans from their own sources, which allows them to ease up on the restrictions a bit. They can also offer more flexible lending terms. In some cases, these portfolios consist of a number of investors who pool their resources together to back real estate investors.

Most banks and lending institutions don't openly advertise that they are portfolio lenders so it can be difficult to locate them. They often obtain their customers through referrals and networking. If you're interested in these lending options, be sure to talk to other investors.

FHA Loans Are Great If They Are Available To You

The Federal Housing Administration, or FHA, insures mortgages for banks so they can feel more confident lending to individuals with lower credit. As an example, health and car insurance work together to mitigate the risk for everyone involved. These loans work in the same way. However, FHA loans are designed to be used on a primary residence so it can be challenging to use it for pure investment properties. The good news is properties with up to four units qualify for FHA loans as long as you plan to live in one of the units.

One of the greatest benefits of choosing an FHA loan is the amount required for a down payment is much lower. In fact, individuals can get a loan for as little as three-and-a-half percent. This helps those who haven't been able to save up the full down payment so they can get started on owning a home or investing in property much faster. The biggest issue with an FHA loan is you must also purchase private mortgage insurance, otherwise known as PMI. This monthly payment exists until the equity in your home rises to the 20 percent threshold. This will increase your mortgage payments and can cut into your cash flow.

203K Loans – Don't Hear About These Much

A subset of the FHA loans, 203K loans are categorized as those given to potential homeowners looking for fixer-upper properties. This type of loan also allows buyers to roll the financing for these rehabilitations into the loan itself. These loans offer the same low down payment as FHA loans and can be used on homes with up to four units as long as the investor intends to live in one of them. Private mortgage insurance also applies.

HomePath Mortgages Are Also Unique

HomePath Mortgages are also backed by the government and were designed to help revitalize non-performing loans into profitable loans. These loans also qualify for lower down payments, which are typically higher than FHA loans. However, individuals who qualify for these loans aren't required to pay for private mortgages. Like the 203K loans, investors can roll repair costs into the amount. These loans are only available on homes that have been repossessed by a bank. HomePath website can help investors find properties that qualify.

Owner Financing – Seller Carry-Back

Some homeowners who are eager to get rid of their homes may agree to owner financing, also known as a 'Seller Carryback Loan.' Instead of making your payment to the bank, you would pay it to the previous owner, essentially renting the home until you own it. However, most sellers will only be willing to do this if they already own the home and don't have a mortgage on it. If there is an existing loan on the home, it must be paid when ownership of the home changes hands or the property will face foreclosure.

All mortgages and other home loans are typically underwritten with a clause that states existing lenders can call for payment in full of the note at the time of a sale – Due on Sale Clause. If the money can't be repaid, they have the right to foreclose on the home. However, some investors are willing to overlook this clause and hope the lender doesn't call back the loan and attempt to foreclose.

Under the right conditions, owner financing can be a suitable method of purchasing properties without relying on banks and other lending institutions. This can also be a useful tool when you are trying to resell the properties you invest in. We will discuss this further when we cover exit strategies.

Hard Money Loans – Have Mixed Reputations

Sometimes business and individuals want to get involved in real estate investing but don't want to do the work required. With the right plan, you can enjoy their financial backing while building your real estate investment business. Some of the characteristics of hard money lending include:

- Dependency on the property's value

- A loan term of six to 36 months

- High interest rates

- Increased loan points

- No income verification

- No credit references required

- No personal credit report

- Deals completed within days

Hard lending may be the right choice for short-term situations, such as when you intend to flip a home and resell it. However, you may find yourself in a difficult situation if the terms of your loan run out before you are able to resell it. You should have several exit strategies in place just in case this occurs.

If you're interested in finding a hard money lender, consider the following resources:

- Talk to your real estate agent or broker;

- Ask someone else who flips homes for lending resources;

- Check the newspaper (some localities);

- Look on Craigslist, LinkedIn, Google+;

- Talk to a mortgage broker; and

- Search online.

Private Money – Shooosh!

Similar to hard money lending, private money comes from individuals who are interested in investing in real estate without involvement in the work. They prefer a more passive income from the venture and need someone who can handle the other elements. Private money lenders are also often less structured than hard money lenders. In most cases, investors have a closer relationship with these lenders prior to asking for funding. Private money lenders also typically require fewer points and fees and can have flexible payment terms to meet everyone's needs.

When private lenders offer money to help back your investments, they will require a specific interest rate in exchange. Just like banks and larger lending institutions, they will hold a mortgage or promissory note on the home, allowing them to foreclose if you fail to make your payments. These lenders will create a similar structure to a bank loan, requiring the interest rate to be set ahead of time over a period ranging from six months to 30 years.

For private lenders, the money is made through the interest rate set. They don't own an equity stake in the amount of cash flow you generate over the period of the loan. In most cases, you will receive funding from one solitary provider, but there are exceptions. Many investors choose this lending option when they foresee an increase in the value of the property over a short period of time, so you can take the profit, refinance the loan and pay back the private lender. Just like hard money lending, it's important to have several exit strategies in place just in case.

Home Equity and Other Lines of Credit

If you have a sizable amount of equity in your primary home, you may want to use this to help fund your investments. Many banks offer an assortment of credit lines, so be sure to talk to the bank that holds your mortgage about which options they offer. If you own your home outright, you may be able to use a variety of banks so ask around. Be wary; banks and other lenders will only loan you a certain percentage of the value of your home, regardless of how much equity you have. This percentage will vary by lender but most of them will cover up to 75-90 percent of the value of your home.

There are many benefits to choosing a home equity loan or line of credit to cover your real estate investment costs. For instance:

▪ The loan is based on the value of your existing residence so there's no need for banks to appraise the home you are trying to buy. This means you can buy a home in poor condition for a low price, flip it and generate a profit.

- The money is yours because it is based off the equity of your home. This allows you to offer cash for your new purchase, which can increase the chances of acceptance.

- There are some tax benefits to these loans. You may be able to deduct the interest paid for the equity borrowed, among other things. Talk to your accountant about the possibilities.

- Interest rates are generally lower because they are backed by your primary residence, and typically are based on the current prime lending rate.

One of the most common ways home equity is used for funding investments is to cover the down payment. The good news is home equity loans are available in both fixed and adjustable rates, giving investors more flexibility in their payments. It's important to consider your goals, financial status and timeline before deciding which home equity product is best for you.

Partnerships Come in All Shapes and Sizes

We've previously discussed partnerships, but one aspect that wasn't covered was their ability to help you finance your investments. For instance, if you have your eye on a piece of property, but it's out of your financial reach, working with a partner who can provide some financial backing can be a valuable asset. In some cases, you may choose to bring in an equity partner for the sole purpose of sharing in the financing. There are several ways you can structure a partnership for the best results. For instance, you may ask your partner to fund the entire purchase while you handle the other aspects of managing the investments or you may only ask for the amount of the down payment. There are no rules for having an equity partner – each deal is different. It's all between the two of you to figure out, especially in terms of how profits will be split, who makes decisions and how to handle specific situations that may arise.

Depending on the partnership agreement you make, your equity partner may be taking a passive role or they may be more active in the process. Having an ownership stake can help your partner have an active role in all aspects of the investment. This also gives them the opportunity to enjoy a percentage of the returns, which may include depreciation, appreciation, cash flow and any profits from the sale of the property.

Equity partners don't receive a set interest rate because they aren't a lender in traditional terms.

Instead, they will receive a set percentage of the returns on the property as agreed upon ahead of time. This encourages a more active role because properties that do well yield a larger profit, while those that struggle may experience a loss. An equity partner is taking a higher risk than private lenders, but the returns have the potential to be much higher. Because it is an operating agreement between partners, there is no risk of foreclosure by the other party.

Commercial Loans Are Specifically For Certain Assets

Most of the options listed above are targeted toward residential properties. However, if you are looking to invest in commercial properties, there is lending available here as well. Even residential properties with more than four units can benefit from a commercial loan rather than a traditional residential loan due to the way they operate.

Commercial loans typically have slightly higher interest rates than residential loans and terms are typically shorter. Lenders often use different qualifiers as well.

Residential loans are geared towards the buyer who typically carries the most weight. However,

commercial loans look more at the value of the property and how much money it can generate. They want to know you can cover the payments if something goes wrong. While they will still look at your personal credit, income and other economic factors, these loans are directed at your financial prowess, rather than your ability to pay. Lenders want to know how much income your new property is capable of generating.

If you need to make renovations or flip a commercial property, these lenders may extend a business line of credit. In some situations, you may qualify for a significant sum, allowing you to flip the property or invest in other areas as well.

Other Financing Options Should Also Be Evaluated

Although not as widely used, there are other opportunities to get the lending you require. Life insurance policies, Roth IRAs, EIULS (401Ks may be used when purchasing a primary residence) and other sources may be available to you. Talk to your financial advisor about what options will suit your needs and help you make your desired investments.

Final Financing Thoughts

There are a vast number of ways you can get the funding you need to start your real estate investment career. One of the most important aspects of being a successful investor is being able to think outside the box and find new ways to move your investments forward. It all starts with understanding your options so you can make the best choices to meet your needs and keep your finances under control. Explore all of your options so you can make necessary changes as your investments move forward.

In addition to being able to get the necessary funding, you will also need to serve as a marketing professional, promoting your business and showing others why they need to invest in you. In the next chapter, we will take a closer look at real estate marketing and help you brainstorm and gather new ideas for maximizing your profits. Marketing will help you not only find funding sources and properties, but can also help you when it's time to rent or sell the properties you own.

7

REAL ESTATE MARKETING

Regardless of the niche and method of real estate investing you choose, you will need to make use of marketing tactics to receive potential funding, locate properties or find renters or buyers. How quickly your business moves forward relies greatly on your ability to reach out to other people and advertise yourself.

You are Your Greatest Asset and You Don't Even Know it

When you get involved in real estate marketing, you need to establish your own personal brand and market yourself. This doesn't have to take a lot of your time and money. This branding can begin as early as when you start talking to people about your interest in real estate investments. These conversations could lead anywhere so it's important to treat each one with the respect and dedication it deserves. This chapter will cover how to effectively build your brand.

YOUR GUIDE TO REAL ESTATE INVESTING

Honesty Is the Best Policy Always

Your brand won't get far if you aren't honest with the people you need to succeed. You don't have to pretend you know everything when you're just starting out. In fact, if you pretend you do, it is one of the fastest ways to ruin your reputation and reduce the chances you will be successful in the future. When you're having conversations, don't be afraid to admit you don't know something. The other person may have valuable insight you can use to learn and grow. Moreover, if you find a topic you don't understand conduct research so you become familiar with the concepts, strategies, and solutions such that the next time this question is posed you will be able to handle it. You may even write a detailed letter to the person who asked you the question in the first place – this touch of professionalism goes a long way.

In addition to admitting what you don't know, don't misrepresent yourself to anyone you talk to. Be proud of your status as a new investor and use that to leverage your growth. While you may not be able to dive into the major deals you're after in the early stages of your career, you will be able to find smaller investments you can use to gain experience and build an operating capital and revenue stream. However, if you do choose to exaggerate or lie about your level of expertise, you will find your investment dreams diminishing when someone discovers the truth.

Build Integrity Every Day

Following through on your promises is essential if you want people to trust you as a brand. This is what will help you build a sense of loyalty in your clients and associates. In the world of investments, people will conduct research on you before making a decision whether or not to work with you. Therefore, you have to make sure your reputation is pristine. Imagine if a lender promised a specific sum to a buyer, only to back out on the deal at the last minute without a valid reason. Chances are they would lose business and may even get sued. Protecting your reputation and keeping your integrity are critical components to your success as an investor.

An Air of Professionalism is Required for Long-Term Success

While some people treat real estate investing as a hobby, if you want it to be a business, you need to treat it as such from the start. Before you build any relationships, make a decision or choose a property to buy, think about it from a business perspective and determine which is the best way to approach it in a professional manner. Create professional business cards and dress

professionally every time you have an opportunity to meet a business contact. Don't forget about the voicemail on the phone you use for your business as well as the condition of your car. Everything about you will be scrutinized before possible partners, funders and investors decide to work with you.

Networking is a Necessity to Build a Successful Foundation

Networking is one of the most essential aspects of marketing and is something you can get started on right away. This method is designed to help you develop relationships that will help you grow both professionally and personally. The good news is it doesn't even have to be a formal effort. Talking to anyone in your day-to-day interactions can quickly become a networking opportunity that improves your business opportunities. While most people think of important business events when they think of networking, this isn't often the case. In fact, when you make networking your lifestyle, you will make great strides in your business.

Impromptu discussions are often the best way to make important contacts you can use o grow your investing business. While it's often ineffective to walk up to just anyone and start talking about your property investments, dropping a quick comment about real estate into a conversation you're already having can quickly generate interest and steer the conversation in that direction.

Networking is often used to help you connect with other people and businesses, but that isn't the only purpose. It's also helpful for building your real estate team. It's difficult to navigate the world of real estate investing on your own and most people can't be successful without

some help. Therefore, it's necessary to use networking to find the right people to work with early on in your venture.

A local real estate investing club can be one of the best places to start your networking. Most major cities have one of these organizations so locate the one closest to you and start attending events. These clubs often meet on a regular basis to discuss local real estate trends, investing strategies and more. You will meet people who have been investing for many years, along with others who are in the earlier stages of their careers. If there are multiple organizations like this in your area, check them all out so you can find the one that best suits your needs and style. It's also important to realize many of these organizations are set up as profit generators, which means you may have to sit through a sales pitch first. However, the ability to connect with other investment professionals can be well worth your time.

If your area doesn't have a real estate investing club or you would prefer to avoid them, there are plenty of other networking opportunities. Find out about landlord association meetings and other live real estate investing events that may take place in your area.

Before you start networking, it's important to have professional business cards you can pass out to the people you meet. Even though many older methods of marketing and networking are no longer used, business cards are still a must-have. Your card should include:

- Your name

- Your company name, if you have one

- Your title

- Your website

- Your telephone number

- Your email address

- The type of investments you make

Online Networking Is Valuable But You Must Be Consistent

Today, there are newer ways to market your business. The Internet has opened new avenues where you can connect with others who may be able to help you along the journey. There are several places you can take advantage of networking online:

- Forums – Real estate investment forums can be the perfect place to ask questions and

get the answers you need. You can also leave comments on other posts to connect with people who may be going through the same issues as you. These websites can be a great place to find people who are willing and able to help you succeed.

- Your Website – It's essential for real estate investors today to have a website they can use to reach more people and share information. It can also be a powerful networking tool. Make sure your website is professional and user friendly to attract a larger target audience. If people are impressed with your website, they are likely to reach out to you.

- Social Media – Social media has become one of the most powerful tools available online. Facebook and Twitter can be a great place to reach out to potential tenants and buyers, while Google+ and LinkedIn can help you grow a professional network. You don't have to start profiles on all of these social media sites in order to be successful. Determine which one will be the most useful to your goals and start there. You can always add more activities later. Social media is all about forming relationships with other people, which can be a valuable marketing and networking tool.

- A Blog – Keeping a blog on your website allows you to share information with your target audience and establish yourself as a leader in your field. Having this level of credibility is invaluable in helping you grow. If you leave commenting open, it will give people the chance to interact with you and potentially become a connection you can rely on.

The Marketing Funnel/Pipeline Is The Mother's Milk Of Real Estate

One of the most critical aspects of marketing to understand is the funnel. The marketing funnel/pipeline refers to the process of guiding your readers and prospects from having no knowledge of what you do to being ready to buy, sell or otherwise take part in your business. This tactic is used in many areas of business and is extremely helpful in real estate investing.

Most people know a funnel is typically used to pour large amounts of liquid into a small space. The top of the funnel/pipeline is wide for easy pouring and it tapers toward the bottom to fit into tight spaces. The marketing funnel works in much the same way. You will first attract a large number of people at the top of the funnel. You will gradually narrow your focus, bringing down only those who fit with your objective.

The tactics you use for your marketing funnel/pipeline will vary based on your goals and the kind of investing you intend to pursue. For instance, a funnel for a wholesaler is going to be vastly different from the one a house flipper may use. One example of a wholesaler funnel/pipeline includes:

- Sending out postcards to area residents who have past due balances on their mortgages

- Setting up a toll-free number for foreclosure assistance

- Connecting that number with a voicemail system for messages

- Calling back those who leave messages

- Meeting with prospective leads and making an offer

- Going through the buying process

- Performing due diligence on the property

- Closing the sale

Each progressive step in this plan becomes a little narrower, helping you find the individuals who are most likely to be willing to sell you their property at a minimum. For instance, you may send out 1,000 postcards and only receive 100 calls from that. Out of those 100 calls, perhaps 15 people leave you a message. After checking into the properties, you may decide to offer on just five of them. Perhaps only a couple of those offers will convert into sales.

This process may seem like a waste of time. After all, reaching out to 1,000 people only to land one or two sales seems a massive misuse of resources. However, this is only one example of a marketing funnel/pipeline. You can adjust yours to best suit your needs, tweaking it and making changes as you go along. As you test your funnel/pipeline, you will get a good idea of your conversion rate, which is the percentage of people who go through the entire process and reach your desired end goal.

Direct Mail Marketing Is A Time Tested Method

One of the older methods of marketing that is still used today is direct mail. These are the advertisements you receive with your regular mail. To effectively use this method, you need to determine who your target audience is and only send ads to these individuals. Regardless of the type of real estate investments you intend to make, you need to have a consistent supply of leads to keep you going. Direct mail can be an effective method of creating a steady number of leads to fill up your funnel/pipeline. In fact, this can be one of your best sources.

How Direct Mail Works – Its Simple

Using direct mail is meant to build awareness in your local community. For most people, they don't buy something the first time they hear about it. They want to know more about the company first. For this reason, you can't send out postcards or other mailers once and stop. Sending these messages multiple times over a period of time will help them become more familiar with your investment business and what you do. Eventually, you will receive responses from a number of the recipients.

Building a List is Critical

Before you start your direct mailing campaign, you need to figure out who needs your products or services. Public records are a great place to start. There are also online companies that can help you locate the people in your area who are most likely to need your help. Because of the rapid changes that take place in the real estate market, it's important to make sure you refresh your list at least once every six months so you aren't sending mailings to people who are no longer in need of your services. It also allows you to add people.

Many Different Types of Direct Mailing

There are essentially two different types of direct mailings most companies use. These include:

- Postcards – Postcards can be created in a variety of sizes to help keep your marketing within your budget. These cards are a good option because they don't require recipients to open an envelope in order to see the information.

- Letter-Sized Postcards – Letter-sized postcards are merely larger than regular postcards. These

cards are a great option because you can put significantly more information on the card.

• Yellow Letters – These direct mailings consist of letters printed on yellow paper and are mailed in an envelope. They are typically addressed in a personal manner and often have a high rate of return.

Direct Mailing Recipients Vary With Your Differing Strategies

The frequency of your mailings and the length of your campaign will vary depending on your marketing goals, including who you want to reach and what investment strategies you will use. Direct mailings can be sent to anyone so you need to pay close attention to what your objectives are. Here are a few groups you may want to target with your efforts:

• Abandoned Properties – There are many reasons people abandon their properties. In most cases, they no longer care enough about the property to do whatever it takes to keep it or don't want to put the money into it. Contact owners of homes that have fallen under obvious disrepair or have been abandoned.

• Foreclosures and Pre-Foreclosures – Foreclosures can often be a great place to find potential investments. Even when these homes are in the early stages of foreclosure, many homeowners are eager to sell quickly. When played correctly, you can provide benefits to the seller as well. Legally, realtors and brokers have to tread lightly when dealing with properties that have been Noticed by a lender – please contact a competent real estate attorney to provide advice in these situations as each state has different statutory guidelines.

• Expired Listings – Real estate agents/brokers have access to all homes listed in the MLS. These listings often have a set expiration date. When the listing expires, these sellers may be willing to accept a lower offer. They also will most likely not have to pay fees to their real estate agent/broker.

• Absentee Owners – Sometimes owners have to relocate for a job or for other reasons and no longer reside in their homes. Contact these owners to determine if they will want to sell.

• Apartment Owners – If apartments are in your investment strategy, sending your mailers to owners of these properties can keep your name in their minds. You don't always have to reach out to distressed proprietors. Sometimes other individuals want to sell their properties and may even be willing to offer seller financing.

• Probates – When individuals pass away, families are often looking to sell the home as quickly as possible. In some cases, they may accept a lower amount for the purchase of the home because they simply want to move on.

Always keep organized records of your marketing campaigns so you can determine whether they are successful and make any necessary adjustments.

Online Advertising Methods Are Varied

More people are turning to the Internet for solutions to their problems. If you aren't taking advantage of these advertising methods, you could be missing a large portion of your target audience. There are many ways you can use the Internet to market yourself. The methods you use will depend greatly on your chosen strategies for your investments. Below, we will discuss several options that will help you make the most of your online advertising efforts.

Facebook and Google Ads are Proven Winners

Facebook and Google are both free to use, but we all know they have to be making money somehow. The answer lies in the advertising space they sell. As an investor, it's worth looking into these advertisements to help reach potential buyers, renters and other business professionals. Even though each of these sites offers ads, there are slight differences. For instance, Google ads target viewers based on what they search, where they are located and what sites they have visited. Facebook, on the other hand, bases ads on location, demographical information, interests and connections.

The best part about these ads is you only pay for when they are used. When you post in the newspaper, you are charged a flat fee, regardless of the outcome. Think about how nice it would be to only pay for the number of people who contact you from your ad. This is how online advertising works. Pay-per-click ads only charge you each time someone clicks on your ad and visits your website.

The Benefits of Pay-per-Click Advertising

1. Target your audience based on location to help draw local customers into your physical business. You will be able to choose exactly what area and distance you want to cover.

2. Facebook ads can be targeted to interests. This social media platform looks at the things users "like" and who their friends are to more effectively reach a target audience. This allows you to show ads only to people who are interested in specific things.

3. Reach certain demographics based on age, gender and other key factors. For instance, you can target individuals who are most likely to be first-time home buyers who live in a specific area to increase your chances of making a sale.

Online Ad Pricing Can Be Tricky

One of the biggest questions you may have is how much it costs to advertise through pay-per-click advertising. In essence, pay-per-click advertising is an auction where those who wish to advertise bid on keywords. When you set up an ad for a specific keyword, it will appear when individuals search that term or it matches their interests. If you bid too low, your ads may not appear often enough to have an impact. However, you will never pay more than you bid. In most cases, you should be able to find a range of prices for specific keyword phrases to help you bid properly. You can set a budget for how much you spend in a given week or month to help keep your costs under control.

Tips for Creating Your Successful Ads

Before you delve into the world of pay-per-click advertising, you need to know how to create the

most effective ads. The following tips will help you get started.

- Ad Destination – Where will your ads lead those who click on them? In most cases, they should go to a dedicated landing page designed to match the topic of the ad.

- An Effective Title – You will have a limited number of characters to use for your title so make them count. Even though your ad will be prominently displayed, you still need to make sure it stands out from any others that may appear at the same time.

- An Enticing Ad – The body of the ad is also essential to your success. You need to appeal to the emotions of your target audience and provide the facts they need to make the right decision. When you interest your audience, you will increase the chances individuals will click on your ads.

- Set a Price – It can be easy to overspend when it comes to pay-per-click advertising. This makes it essential to set not only the price for each click, but also for how much you are willing to spend in a given week or month to help cap your costs.

 YOUR GUIDE TO REAL ESTATE INVESTING

Creating an Effective Landing Page is Critical

While creating a website isn't an absolute necessity, it can be an effective tool in obtaining the leads you are looking for. A telephone number can serve your purpose, but because many people turn to the Internet to find what they need, it's often a better method of gathering new leads. Even if you don't have the expertise or the budget to create a professional landing page, there are templates you can use to get started. Freelancers can also be a cost-effective way to get the landing page you need. A Facebook business page is another free alternative you can use for your landing page, though professional pages are typically more effective.

Final Media and Marketing Thoughts

Real estate marketing is complex, but doesn't have to take a lot of time and money. This chapter is just a brief overview of how to market your real estate investment brand. Each of these elements of marketing can be further expanded upon. There are also additional options available. As you get started, it's best to start working with just one or two strategies before moving on to adding more. Get to know these initial marketing plans first. You may also find some options aren't as effective as others so you may need to make adjustments along the way. Keeping records will ensure you can better track your results.

Up to this point, we have discussed choosing the right niche, getting started as an investor, how to finance your purchase and how to market your business. In the next chapter, we will move on to discuss how to maximize your results and how to properly execute your exit strategy.

8

EXIT STRATEGIES

Real estate investing isn't something most people get into as a hobby. It requires a lot of time and hard work, as well as a large monetary investment, making it a business venture, rather than a hobby. When done properly over time, your real estate investments should create a substantial income that results both from cash flow and appreciation of the properties you purchase. Regardless of whether you intend to resell properties or you want to hold onto them and manage them as rental properties, you need to create and follow exit strategies that help you achieve your goals. This chapter will address these strategies and teach you how to use them to your benefit.

Traditional Real Estate Selling Primer

Just like your typical home buyers, real estate investors can hire real estate agents/brokers and go with more traditional selling strategies. Before you choose an agent, be sure to interview several so you can get a feel for their principles and how they handle sales. It's important to find an experienced real estate agent/broker with a reputation for closing a majority of their sales. A rule of thumb is to hire someone who have been a full-time Realtor for a minimum of 10 years with at least 200+ closed transactions under their belt.

After you choose a real estate agent, you will likely sign a "listing agreement" that states they will earn a commission if they sell one of your properties. They will inform you of everything you need to know to effectively list your properties and why it's important to list with the MLS. This agent can help you choose the most appropriate sale price, keeping it low enough to avoid sitting on the market too long and high enough to make a reasonable profit. A competent agent will compare with similar properties to help you set the right price.

The listing agreement will also detail how much commission your agent is entitled to after a sale. In most cases, this amount equals six percent of the sale price. However, if the buyer is represented by a real estate agent as well, this commission is split between the two agents.

This isn't the end of your work in selling your property. While your agent will handle much of the sales process, there are things you need to do as well. These steps will ensure your property sells as quickly as possible. Fast turnaround is essential for a successful investment venture. This includes making your property as visually appealing as possible on the inside and outside. Looking at other area properties can help you come up with new ideas.

For a single-family home, staging can be a valuable tool to help potential buyers visualize what their own furniture will look like. Be sure you use more than just furniture; add artwork, plants and other decor for the best results. If you specialize in multi-family or commercial properties, make sure they are as occupied as possible and in good operating condition.

Once an offer is made, you will be heavily involved in the negotiation process. Just like

purchasing procedures, you will need to fill out a lot of paperwork that is handled by a title and escrow company. Both parties will need to sign these documents, money will be exchanged and the deal will close, allowing you to continue your investment journey.

For Sale by Owner – The Dreaded FSBO

You don't have to use a real estate agent if you are confident in your knowledge and skills. One of the biggest reasons investors choose this option is the absence of the six percent fee charged by real estate agents. However, it's important to realize what this fee will get you. Competent agents/brokers will:

- Properly strategize with the owner during the preparation period

- Help the owner properly prepare the property for the marketplace

- Assist the owner during disclosure preparation

- Strategize timing for the presentation to the public

- List the property with the MLS, online, social media, etc.

- Place signs in your yard, market the property to all area agents/brokers/neighbors

- Show the property whenever someone wants to see it

- Obtain offers, properly counsel the owner on the status of offers

- Manage the negotiations, continue to advise the owner

- Handle the contract paperwork, keep detailed file

- Make sure escrow is completed with a complete document compilation

There are many more things that are performed by a competent and experienced agent – the list would go on for several pages including the numerous hours spent on the phone with the owner, contractors, vendors, agents, escrow officers, appraisers, and on-and-on. Most people do not appreciate the efforts competent and experienced agents go through with each transaction.

For those investors who feel this fee is too high, selling by themselves can be a great option. However, you need to understand your property won't be listed with the MLS and thus won't get much of the exposure real estate can get. This means you will need to do more work to market your properties to buyers.

Seller Financing Might Help Deal Work

In some situations, the seller is willing to continue carrying the mortgage, allowing the buyer to pay them directly instead of applying for their own mortgage. There are a number of reasons investors around the world are using this method of selling a property. In this agreement, the seller

works as the bank and extends a loan of sorts to the buyer. Like a traditional mortgage, the buyer will make a down payment and then continue to cover mortgage for the life of the loan or until they choose to move on and sell.

Why Use Seller Financing?

While there are many reasons individuals may choose this method of financing a home, the most common reason is for home buyers who may not qualify for a traditional mortgage. Because of the economic downturn and subsequent housing market crash, it has become more difficult for individuals to get the bank financing they need to buy a home. Some people are unable to document their income or are self-employed, while others may have blemishes on their credit report that make lending difficult.

This may be the most common reason for seller financing, but it isn't the only way sellers can benefit. Many investors choose this option because it provides them a source of monthly income they wouldn't otherwise generate, similar to renting out a property. However, because the buyer is actually purchasing the home, there is no maintenance, tenants or rental issues to deal with. The property becomes the sole responsibility of the buyer, including all the rights and expenses, such as property taxes and repair costs.

Other sellers choose to use this type of financing to help with tax issues at the end of an investment career. Not everyone stays in the real estate investment game for their entire lives. However, liquidating properties can come with heavy tax implications. Seller financing can provide a steady income and eliminate some of these tax problems. Consult a tax attorney, CPA, or other licensed tax advisor before making this decision.

How is Seller Financing Used and Who Benefits Most?

If you choose this exit strategy, you need to request a significant, non-refundable down payment to protect the seller and reduce the risks the buyer will stop making monthly payments. A higher down payment means a lower risk to sellers. Buyers aren't afraid to lose smaller amounts of money. Even if you are handling the financing yourself, make sure you follow all the other steps of a traditional sale, such as using a title and escrow service, attorneys and the proper paperwork.

Who Can Use Seller Financing?

In most cases, seller financing is only available when the seller owns the home outright and there is no existing mortgage in place. If you already have a mortgage on the property through a lending institution, they will want the balance of your account at the time of the sale because of the "due on sale" clause found in most contracts.

After you sell your property, you may choose to sell the mortgage to another investor at any time. This creates a note buying strategy investors can use to obtain properties that will immediately begin generating an income.

What Are the Risks?

The biggest risk you will have when using this exit strategy is buyers who fail to make their monthly payments as promised. Fortunately, you can still put the home through the foreclosure process if this does occur. However, this can be an expensive, extensive, and difficult process. You will need to hire an experienced real estate attorney to help you through the foreclosure process to protect yourself and your investment. Once the foreclosure is complete, you will again own the home and can resell it to another buyer.

You can never completely avoid the risk of foreclosure, regardless of what you do, but you can minimize those risks. Screen your buyers carefully to evaluate potential risk factors. Asking for higher down payments can also reduce your risks because buyers are more vested in the property from the start.

Lease/Purchase Options Can Be Useful

Investors may also offer lease options as a viable exit strategy for investment properties. There are typically two parts to this: the lease and the option. A lease, just like any other rental agreement, means a tenant will move into the home and makes present monthly payments.

However, unlike your typical rental agreement, this lease comes with an option. This means the tenant will have the legal right to purchase the home at a pre-determined price within a set amount of time. During this period of time, the investor will not be able to put the property up for sale to anyone else. These agreements typically require the tenant to pay a fee for the right to this option. The fee can typically be applied toward the purchase price if the tenant chooses to exercise it.

The lease option also provides help for the seller. It is often a great alternative for investors who are having difficulty selling a property straight out but don't want to discount the price. With a lease option, the seller wins in all situations, whether the tenants choose to exercise the option to purchase, the tenants choose to stay on as renters or the investor receives the opportunity to sell to someone else at a future date.

Advantages of Lease Options

There are several advantages to using the lease option as an exit strategy.

▪ A Short-Term Solution for a Slow Market – The current housing market makes it difficult to flip homes and turn a profit. Choosing a lease option for these situations can provide a steady flow of income and gives the seller a chance to find a buyer in a better market.

▪ Lease Option Candidates Take Care of Property – One of the biggest concerns landlords have is whether their tenants will care for the property. Lease option tenants typically are more responsible with small repairs and other maintenance because they often plan to purchase the home.

▪ No Real Estate Commission – Unless you use a real estate agent to find a potential buyer, you will be able to sell without owing a commission. You can often fetch a higher selling price due to the flexibility you offer and you will save yourself the six percent fee.

Disadvantages of Lease Options

Like most areas of real estate investing, there are some distinct disadvantages to choosing lease options as your exit strategy.

▪ The Danger of "Due on Sale" – Even though no sale is technically made when the lease option is first created, it can still cause issues with the "due on sale" clause. Banks can trigger this clause on a lease option because there is still a transfer of property, even in the absence of a sale. While it can be challenged in court, lenders are free to exercise this clause if they choose.

▪ You Can't Sell to Anyone Else – Once someone is in the home on a lease option, you are locked into their residency for the period of the option. Even if the market improves, you won't be able to offer the home for sale until after this time period has passed.

▪ You Could Be Sued – There have been instances where investors were sued by tenants for equity in a home they lived in on a lease option. There is typically little chance for tenants to win these cases, it still can cost investors valuable time and money going to court and fighting the case.

Regardless of whether you choose to offer a lease option, it's important to realize few tenants actually purchase the home. Unfortunately, many investors have used this to their advantage and abused this exit strategy by taking on tenants who would never qualify for a mortgage or by charging high fees or down payments, on the hope tenants won't buy. This can leave tenants in bad shape in the end. These practices should not be used by any investor who wishes to invest with integrity.

1031 Exchanges

Selling property typically comes with taxes, just like any other method of earning cash. Chances are you will be charged a significant amount upon the sale of your properties. However, there are ways to defer the taxes owed to help you move your investment venture forward more quickly.

To take part in this tax deferment, you must follow a few simple rules, allowing you to reuse the funds for investing further. This is the government's way of helping investors put money back into the economy. To ensure you can take advantage of this tax deferment, make sure you talk to an experienced professional before making any decisions.

The Golden Strategy – IRC 121 + IRC 1031 & Legally Avoiding Capital Gains Taxes

Many of our parent's friends who have fortunately accumulated significant equity in their homes over the last several decades are faced with a dilemma of downsizing into a smaller home because they can no longer conveniently or adequately take care of their properties. Importantly, many of them desire a simpler-smaller property, usually all single-level, accessible and easy to maintain. The problem exists because if they sell their home with substantial equity they face significant capital gains exposure even with the IRC Section 121 exclusion in place.

For example, a married couple may exclude from capital gains tax $500,000 (Sec. 121) if they have resided in their primary residence two (2) out of the last five (5) years. So, if a couple has accumulated $2,000,000 in equity in their home (after improvements and original pur-

chase price) they would still have a $1,500,000 capital gain. In California, with all of the taxes included, the capital gains rate is approximately 33% (highest in U.S.). Thus, this couple would have to pay approximately $495,000 in capital gains taxes in the next tax year after their sale. So how do we get around this challenge?

Congress Is On Your Side Sometimes – Believe It or Not

With the Congressional enactment of the American Jobs Creation Act of 2004 and the Housing and Economic Recovery Act of 2008, and Department of the Treasury Revenue Procedure 2008-16 the government has made it easier for homeowners to keep more of their equity – and even not pay any capital gains taxes, ever – if they don't want to.

Internal Revenue Code Section 121 (The "121 Exclusion")

This code section says that if a property is your primary residence and you (or you and your spouse) have lived in it for two (2) out of the last five (5) years you can sell the property and exclude from taxes $250,000 if you are single, or $500,000 if you are married and file a joint tax return. This code does not apply to second homes, vacation homes, rental homes, or investment properties. Another wrinkle is that you can only exclude capital gains and not recaptured depreciation (but that is another article).

Internal Revenue Code Section 1031 (The "1031 Exchange")

A 1031 exchange allows a person to sell a property ("relinquished property") that was held as a rental or investment property and then exchange the proceeds from that sale

WHAT IS | A 1031 EXCHANGE?

A real estate transaction that allows you to defer taxes when you exchange "LIKE-KIND" BUSSINESS, INCOME OR INVESTMENT PROPERTIES.

into a new "like-kind" property ("replacement property") also to be held as a rental or investment property. The benefit of using a 1031 exchange is that no matter what capital gains you may have accumulated in the "relinquished" property they are all transferred into the "replacement" property and no taxes are due or payable at that time. The taxes are deferred into the replacement property. The 1031 exchange does not apply to a primary residence, but you can convert your primary residence into a rental property and take advantage of all its benefits.

Combining IRC Section 121 and IRC Section 1031 Is Powerful

Over the 239 years or so that this country has existed there has never been one set of laws that allowed more American families to accumulate more wealth than Section 1031. Mind-boggling multi-generational wealth has been created by clever investors who never pay capital gains taxes on their real estate portfolios even though they keep selling and buying more and more and bigger and bigger buildings.

With careful and meticulous tax planning people can combine both IRC 121 and 1031 to legally avoid and/or defer all capital gains taxes on the sales of real property – while improving the assets by buying bigger and better buildings each time one is sold.

Three Different Methods of Converting Properties for this Strategy

There are three (3) distinct transactions which these two code sections will allow sellers/ investors to take full advantage of the code.

• (1) Rental Property Converted to a Primary Residence (no prior 1031 exchange)

If you bought an investment/rental property and later wanted to convert it to a primary residence you will have to move into the property for a minimum of 2 years to qualify for IRC 121. There are some other restrictions but the main benefits of 121 + 1031 are still available to you.

• (2) Rental Property Converted to a Primary Residence (prior 1031 exchange)

This case is similar to 1 above. The difference is that the original purchase of the investment property was done with a 1031 exchange. The minimum time you will have to own this property is five years to qualify for IRC 121 exclusion and then you can 1031 exchange it again. You do not have to live it in for five years, but only two out of the last five years. There are some other restrictions but the main benefits of 121 + 1031 are still available to you in this fact pattern.

• (3) Primary Residence Converted to a Rental Property - The Golden Strategy

This is the golden strategy that applies to many people. The Internal Revenue Service drafted Revenue Procedure 2005-14 which allows you to move out of your primary residence and convert it into a rental property. Although there is no rule or statute it is common practice that a person should rent the converted property for a minimum of one year (I always say a year and a day with full intention of making it a rental). The year and a day rule of thumb cures the primary residence into a "rental/investment" property. Now you can sell the rental/investment property and take advantage of IRC 121 ($500,000 exclusion) and 1031 exchange the property into another, more profitable or desirable building – thus deferring any leftover capital gains exposure.

But Where Am I Going To Live?

When we talk to people about this strategy the first question they always ask is "[W]here am I going to live? The answer is "[A]nywhere you want to." A person can take the proceeds of the rental income from their newly converted rental property and go and rent somewhere else for the 12 or so months why the property is "curing." In fact, most of the time the rental/investment property will kick-out substantial rental income such that the owner can find suitable rentals and still have left over monies each month (more than likely their mortgage obligations on their primary residence is exhausted).

We tell our clients to look for something to rent on a golf course, a simple single-level condominium, or a beautiful unit in a high-rise building. There are so many different options all of which can be afforded by the budget from the rental income.

What Will I Buy with the 1031 Exchange Proceeds?

We have always counseled clients to look for a commercial building or a mixed use building to exchange into. Well positioned commercial buildings will typically have tenants on triple-net leases where the tenant is paying more than 100% of the actual expenses of the building including property taxes, insurance, improvements, etc.

If you purchase a building with greater value than the proceeds from the relinquished property just make sure the amount of rental income will be enough to cover your expenses.

A mixed use building with retail and residential components are attractive because the owner may decide to live in one of the residential units.

The ultimate answer is it really doesn't matter. There are so many opportunities that exist the possibilities are endless.

Step By Step Procedure Looks Like This

Step 1. Accumulated Equity Above $1,500,000

Step 2. Move out and convert primary residence to rental for a year and a day

Step 3. Find rental for you to live in with proceeds from renting your previous primary residence

Step 4. After 12 months or so sell the rental/investment "relinquished" property to take advantage of Sec.121

Step 5. 1031 exchange the proceeds of the relinquished rental sale into a new building

Step 6. Identify "replacement" property within 45 days of the sale and close escrow within 180 days of sale of "relinquished" property

Step 7. Continue to rent at your discretion – or find a new rental – or move into the "replacement" property

Step 8. Enjoy the benefits of keeping your assets within your family and plan to keep the "replacement" property in the family succession

Many people have accumulated significant equity in their homes over the last several decades and now they are looking to downsize but are faced with this problem. This problem exists for thousands of retiring baby boomers (especially in the San Francisco Bay Area). We have now shown you tools that the government has given us which affords us an opportunity to keep all of our assets without having to pay any capital gains taxes. This is not a complicated strategy, but it does require due diligence, patience, and a desire to accomplish your goals. Hiring a real estate professional to help you through this process is key.

CONCLUSION – FINAL THOUGHTS

You should now have a clear picture of how to handle exit strategies so you can get rid of your investments when you are ready to make a profit. It's important to have the end in sight to make sure everything goes smoothly.

Throughout this guide, we have covered most general topics of information that you will need to know to get started in real estate investing – however there are many things that may arise during your ownership, transactions, and real estate experience that will be slightly different, dynamic, and nuanced. We explored what investing means and what you can expect from getting involved in this field. We then continued to learn about what you should do to prepare yourself before getting involved, what strategies and niches you have to choose from and how to lay the groundwork with a solid business plan.

You should now know how to look for the best investment properties, how to finance those purchases, how to market yourself and how to choose and implement an exit strategy.

When you put these plans into practice, you will find you can make the most of your real estate investment venture, turning a profit and taking pride in the business you are trying to build. It is paramount that you treat your investment properties as individual businesses and if they somehow don't turn out profitable, then find a way to turn them around or relinquish them and start over.

If you ever have questions please do not hesitate to reach out to us – we are here to help.

ABOUT THE AUTHORS

Shelly Roberson

After Shelly Roberson graduated from UC Berkeley she started full-time in real estate at the age of 22 in title and escrow. Shelly received her real estate license at age 23 and began representing buyers and sellers. Shelly has been a licensed realtor since 1992 and she has successfully closed 700+ transactions. Shelly brings a wealth of skill, experience and professionalism to her trade that is unrivaled. Shelly is incredibly detail oriented and a savvy negotiator. In addition to providing sage real estate counsel to her clients Shelly designs, remodels, and sources vendors for her clients at no charge – just as part of her value-added services. We are unaware of any other Realtor who provides these comprehensive services at the level Shelly does.

www.shellyroberson.com
www.shellyrobersonrealtor.com
Email: shellyroberson@gmail.com
Phone: 1-650-464-3797

David S. Roberson, Esq

David S. Roberson, Esq. is a licensed real estate attorney, a licensed real estate broker, and has been involved in the real estate business since he graduated from college in 1986. David has personally been involved in hundreds of real estate transactions, has personally inspected over 2,500 residential properties, 12 million square feet of new commercial space, and is an expert in 12 separate building code categories. David and his wife Shelly have managed a personal portfolio of real properties in California and Arizona since 1998. David is currently the principal broker/owner of Silicon Valley Property Management Group and manages over 100+ residential and commercial properties for clients.

www.svpmg.net
Email: droberson.esq@gmail.com
Phone: 1-408-838-5113